It Seems Like Yesterday

THE SECRET TO LIFE
IS KNOWING HOW IT WILL END

Robert Rodriguez Jr

Copyright © 2021 by Robert Rodriguez Jr

All rights reserved. No part of this book may be reproduced or used in any manner without written permission of the copyright owner except for the use of quotations in a book review.

Imprint: Rocky the Lion Press

Library of Congress Cataloging-in-Publication Data
Control number: 2020924848
It Seems Like Yesterday: The secret to life is knowing how it will end/Robert Rodriguez Jr

Paperback ISBN 978-1-7363403-0-1

Ebook ISBN 978-1-7363403-1-8

Available on Audible

TO MY SIS

1

First Night

I watched them lift him off the hospital bed, slide him onto a gurney, and strap him in. His eyes were open but just there for the ride; nothing that was happening seemed to register. We followed the gurney as they wheeled him down the long corridor, a path it had traveled many times. His hands were folded on his chest. He seemed comfortable. I wasn't, though. I was in new territory.

As two large doors swung open, the gurney made its way over the threshold headed toward the transport vehicle. Its back doors were open, waiting for its next passenger. I watched the wheels collapse on the gurney as it slid onto the van with two loud clunks. He disappeared as the doors closed.

Uncertainty is something you never get used to. You tell yourself that you can handle anything, but the truth is, life is tricky. It puts you in situations you've never really thought of or could ever prepare for.

I followed the transport vehicle the best I could. I knew exactly where it was going, but I didn't want to lose sight of it. The cargo it carried was important to me. As I drove down the road my mind raced, thinking about all the different things happening at the same time. The underlying sentiment I felt was just when you think you have everything figured out: everything changes.

The drive was from Visalia, California to Lindsay, a small town between Fresno and Bakersfield. I turned off Highway 137 onto Tulare Avenue in Lindsay and followed the transport vehicle into a parking lot. It pulled up to the double doors in front of the building and stopped. I walked over and waited as they slid him out on the gurney with the same two clunks it made going in.

He was asleep until the gurney's wheels dropped to the pavement. His eyes opened, but seemed lost. He looked at me with no emotion, just questions. The two front doors opened and swallowed him as they had many others. The lobby was full of people, some in wheelchairs, some sitting on sofas and chairs.

I followed the gurney in, looking around at the people as it made its way through the lobby and down a long hallway. I was shocked. People in wheelchairs lined the walls on both sides. Some were slouched forward; some were leaning sideways with their mouths open looking at the ground; and others were reaching out, asking me to take them home or to show them where their room was. It looked like a fifty-car pileup on the highway with all the casualties waiting to be rescued.

We were in a nursing home. *I'm a heel!* I thought. *How could I bring my dad to a place like this? What kind of son am I?* A million thoughts raced through my mind. I was in a land I had never considered coming to, as a patient or as a visitor. We weren't home anymore, and Dorothy wasn't here to click her heels and take us there.

That day is etched in my mind. It's like September 11, 2001. We all remember exactly where we were, who we were with, and how we felt. We can't forget.

On May 20, 2014, life changed, never to be the same because it marked the day Dad's life would change forever. He had turned down a road that only leads to decline. And that same road was my path, not on a gurney, not as a patient, but as a son.

There are two absolutes in our lives that are guaranteed: the day we're born and the day we die. At funerals you hear the old cliché — I hate even saying it, it's so worn out. But here it goes: They say it's not the day we were born or the day we die, it's what we did with the dash in between. The good we did, friends we had and what people will remember us by. But there's a whole other world of things that happen while we walk along that skinny little dash. There are countless surprises, joys, tragedies, triumphs, and failures. This book is about that flat, straight, bumpy, jagged, sometimes unbearable line that Dad traveled from September 27, 1935 until...

2

Where it all Began

Sixto Rodriguez was born in 1898 in Chihuahua Mexico. In 1910 the Mexican Revolution began, and at an unknown date Sixto joined Pancho Villa in the uprising of the people against the corrupt government. He fought with him for five years. After the revolution, he came back to Chihuahua to live with his grandfather on his ranch.

On a dark hot summer's night in 1920, he heard a noise in the barn. He made his way there and found two men coming toward him. He picked up a pitchfork and killed them both. It's unclear who the men were, or what they were doing there, but not long after the incident the authorities were looking for him. I'm not sure if it was because he killed the two men or for some other reason. But I do know that he fled the country and crossed into the United States.

Margarita Peñalver was born on December 10, 1908 in Sinaloa, Mexico. Shortly after her birth, her mother,

Maria, carried her across the Rio Grande to the United States, leaving a country she loved in hopes of a better life for her child.

Sixto and Margarita met and married in Delano, California where they started a family. On September 27, 1935 at 4 a.m. they would have their fourth child, a son: Roberto Peñalver Rodriguez.

They eventually became a family of six: five boys and one girl. In order from oldest to youngest they were Teddy, Gloria, Marcos, Roberto, Steve, and Arthur.

In my first draft of this chapter I tried to only use Dad's name, Roberto, when referring to him because I wasn't born yet. But I can't do it; it just doesn't feel right. So, from this point on when I use the term "Dad," I'm referring to Roberto Peñalver Rodriguez, my father.

Dad's earliest memory was of being in a cotton field, sitting on a cotton sack, with the sun beating down on him. He was no more than two years old. The sacks were up to sixteen feet in length back then. He remembers watching his mom picking the cotton, sweating, and dragging him along on the sack while she picked. He said it was a good memory, that it reminded him of how hard it was to keep food on the table back then and how hard his mother worked.

He remembered being in Coalinga and Cutler, California for grape season. They didn't have housing to sleep in. "The big trees that surrounded the grape fields were our cover," he said, "and the mosquitoes were vicious."

He was five or six years old at the time and remembered having fun because the whole family migrated together, no matter where they went. And everyone worked. Regardless of how small you were, you contributed. They picked anything that was in season, wherever that might be.

But life wasn't easy for Dad, especially his first few years. He was born with a club foot, and when his father, Sixto, drank, he either wanted to kill him or cut off his crooked foot. Dad said he remembered his dad telling his mom he was defective. Not like a defective car part, but a defective human being, not worthy of walking on this earth. I could tell it hurt him to think about it. I wondered what kind of man, what kind of father, what kind of person does that to a child.

He said whenever his dad drank and started staring at him, his mom would hide him in a cupboard or tell him to go hide somewhere outside until he sobered up. Dad said that lasted until he was about five or six years old.

All of Dad's family feared him when he drank, like a kid that fears the dark. But Dad said he could be good when he was sober. I wondered how he could say that. How could he ever feel Sixto was a good father? But I guess that's what kids do when they have a bad parent. They look for the good to try and minimize the reality of the bad.

Dad told me that when Sixto was good, he would tell them stories of fighting with Pancho Villa. He told them of one of the battles against the federal troops. He said the flag bearer got killed and the Mexican flag fell to the ground, and he heard someone call out, "*Muchacho! Recogé la bandera!* (Pick up the flag!)" It was Pancho Villa calling out to him. He said he picked up the flag and continued toward the federal troops.

I can't say that any of the above paragraph is true, but that's what he told Dad. I didn't want to put it in this chapter, because I didn't want to make it seem like I was glorifying him in any way. He doesn't deserve it. But because Dad said it, I wrote it.

The biggest problem with Sixto was that Dad, and the rest of his family, never really knew what kind of father, or husband, they were going to have on any given day. He was like a Dr. Jekyll and Mr. Hyde.

When Dad was eight or nine years old, Sixto went out drinking with some friends and flipped the car he was driving. He had a bad concussion and probably damage to his brain. It would mark the beginning of him losing his mind, something that actually started years before. Dad's older brother Marcos's oldest son Fernando has done extensive research on our family history. He traveled to Mexico to meet Sixto's relatives that were still living. They told him that there was something wrong with him, that they knew from a young age he was different.

They found him one day after the accident wandering around with no clothes on in public. They arrested him and he was evaluated and committed to Camarillo State Hospital for the insane. (An odd fact: When Camarillo State Hospital closed its doors in 1997, it became Channel Islands State University, which my son would eventually graduate from with a biology degree).

I asked Elizabeth, my uncle Marcos's oldest daughter, if my uncle ever told her anything about Sixto. She said there was one story he told her a few times that upset him every time he retold it. I mentioned earlier that they all worked, that nobody stayed home, and everyone was part of the work force. But what I didn't mention was that when Dad and all the brothers got paid for their work, their dad would take all the money from them and go to the bar and buy rounds of drinks for the other men in the bar. He would waste the money meant for food and clothes for the family. Both Elizabeth and Fernando said their dad never forgave him for that. He couldn't get the fact that they didn't have clothes, shoes, or food on the table and his father couldn't care less.

Sixto was let out after six months and came back to Delano. It didn't take long for him to start drinking again and wreak havoc in their home. One day he was hitting Grandma Margarita, and they called the police. They picked him up and put him in road camp for six months. When he got out, he didn't last long. He started telling the family there were bombs under their beds. Every day he got farther and farther from reality, until one day, after they called the police again, he was arrested. He was evaluated again and was sent to Modesto State Hospital, where he would spend most of his remaining life.

From that day forward, it was Grandma Margarita, Dad, his four brothers, and his sister Gloria left to survive on their own. But at least they knew the person they feared the most wouldn't be there to torment them and squander the money meant to keep the family fed and clothed.

3

Surviving

Dad and his brothers knew that money was the key to their survival, and that they had to do whatever it took to make money. Grandma Margarita cleaned and diced cactus leaves (*nopales*) and would put them in a big pot, then Dad would put them in a wagon and go door to door selling them for five cents a cup. It doesn't sound like much, but everything mattered back then. It's hard for us to appreciate it nowadays. We might not even pick a nickel up if it was lying on the ground. It's insignificant. But to them, it was a big part of their next meal.

They did anything they could to survive. They picked cotton, potatoes, and anything else they could pull from the ground or off a branch. My uncle Arthur, Dad's youngest brother, told me that they picked cotton and would pick from 250 to 500 pounds of cotton every day. Dad shined shoes outside the local bars. He said the number one question he got from his customers was

"Do you have a sister?" He sold tamales at the bars in the evening to their customers. The bar owners would try to kick him out, but the patrons would tell them, "We'll leave if you don't let him sell his tamales."

Most people don't feel like their next meal is at stake every day, but that's how Dad's family felt most of the time. They had seven mouths to feed seven days a week, and every day was the same. There wasn't enough money.

Dad's younger brother, my uncle Steve, told me their house was tiny. There was no bathroom inside, only an outhouse out back. It had a wood-burning cooking stove inside, where, Dad told me, Grandma Margarita would make some type of small cakes that he loved. They all slept in one small bedroom with four small beds packed close together.

Grandma Margarita not only had to make sure they ate every day, she had to keep them in line and discipline them. Dad told me she had a thick leather strap, the ones barbers used to sharpen their razors. My uncles Steve and Arthur both told me about the strap. They remembered it clearly. It hung on a big nail by the front door, and that was where they liked to see it. If it wasn't there, that meant someone was getting a whipping. Dad said she would bend them over and whack the heck out of whoever was being punished. He said she didn't do it just for the heck of it either. They could be pretty wild and deserved it most of the time.

She made them take a bath once every two weeks. It was a luxury – I guess. Grandma Margarita would fill a tin tub up and make each one take a bath, from oldest to youngest. My uncle Steve said they had one towel, so by the time it got to the youngest's turn, the towel was soaked and the water was almost black. It's a story I would make a connection to later in my life.

They made the best of their lives. They learned to make their own toys. They would go to the junk yard and find what they needed to make wagons and scooters out of old skates with metal wheels. They made rubber-band guns; they made kites out of sticks, string, flour, and newspaper. I know they flew because Dad showed me how to make one when I was a kid, and it flew like the ones bought at the store.

Dad finished his freshman year in high school and decided it was time to leave home. At fourteen he moved to Camarillo, California and stayed with Tia (aunt) Martina, who was Grandma Margarita's sister. I was lucky enough to know her. She was always cooking and always had a smile on her face. A beautiful person.

Dad learned to pick oranges. He said he picked fifty boxes a day for sixteen cents a box. He tried to pay his aunt rent, but she wouldn't take it. He picked broccoli in the rain and trimmed lettuce with a small hoe. He said it was back-breaking work.

I always wondered why he quit school. He only had three more years and he would have had his high school diploma. That was like having a college degree back then. But one day Dad told me a story. He said that one day he went off to school like any other day but would soon find out it wasn't just any other day. He said he walked up to his house after school and nobody was there. The front door was wide open, and everything was gone inside. His mom and everyone else were gone.

I always felt that must have been terrible. How could

everybody in his family pack up and leave and not tell him. Why didn't he find them in town and live wherever they had moved? I asked him if he found them. He said he did, but it was time for him to leave. He never told me what really happened and why they moved or why he left Delano, but I knew something happened that he just didn't want to tell me.

But knowing Dad's life from that point forward, I would say it was the catalyst that propelled him toward all the good and everything else life would put in his path. His life was his own and from then on, every decision was his. He would make the choices for his own future. But there was one thing he didn't consider, one thing most don't account for that doesn't require anyone's permission to alter someone's plans: the ever-powerful unpredictability of life.

A Note:
Grandpa Sixto

I remember traveling to go see Sixto at Modesto State Hospital when I was about six or seven. It's the only time I remember seeing him. He was sitting on a picnic bench with a grey shirt, khaki pants, and a hat on. I don't remember ever talking to him, or him talking to me either.

In 1970 Modesto State Hospital closed its doors. Sixto was brought back to Delano and put in a home. I called my cousin Elizabeth and asked her if she remembered seeing him when she was young. She remembered her parents bringing him to their house from the home a couple of times. She said she remembered his stare most of all. It was a stare of nothingness. She said he never uttered a word. "He was definitely checked out," she said.

Fernando, my uncle Marcos's son, told me of a time he came to their house. My aunt, Tia Lupe, was in the backyard and Sixto was at their house. He said Sixto came out of the house and walked up and told her that he had a beautiful bird for her. Leery of what he was talking about, she just said: "That's nice." He reached into his jacket pocket and pulled out a dead bird in the palm of his hand. My aunt picked up the bird and told him how beautiful it was, just to get out of the situation. She told my uncle Marcos that she didn't want him at their house anymore because she feared for the kids. That would be the last time he would come to their house.

He wandered away from the home one hot summer's day and was found a few days later. He was on the side of Highway 99 by the railroad tracks in Delano. It was over a hundred degrees that day, Dad said. He was wearing a jacket and had lit a fire to keep warm. He died from exposure a few hours later.

Grandma Margarita

I didn't know Grandma Margarita very well. I remember her telling me hi when we would go visit, which was not too often. We lived in San Jose and she lived in Delano. And I can't speak to the person she was, only what dad told me and what I could learn from family. But I do know she must have been tough and loved her family to survive an abusive husband and still be able to raise a large family alone.

My cousins Elizabeth and Fernando knew her in a way I didn't. They each spent a lot more time with her growing up in the same town and have good memories of her and the person she was. I wish I could have known her better.

4

The Military

Dad eventually made it back to Delano and did whatever work he could find until he decided to join the Army. He and a couple of friends went to Fresno to the induction center to see about joining. The recruiter asked him if he wanted to go into the airborne division.

"What's that?" he asked.

"You'll jump out of planes," the recruiter said.

"I don't think I would like to do that," he said.

"Don't worry, once you get to your regular outfit you can tell them you don't want to be a paratrooper."

It wasn't true. Once he signed his enlistment papers and they were stamped with the word airborne, that was his only choice, there was no backing out.

After his physical he was sent on a bus to Fort Ord, California for basic training. It was eight weeks of basic, and eight weeks of advanced training. After he finished he flew to Fort Campbell, in Kentucky, and was assigned to his regular outfit, the 11th Airborne Division, and placed in the 508th ARCT Regiment. Once he started his training, he knew he couldn't quit because there were three guys in training from his hometown Delano. The whole town would know he chickened out. He went through jump school and earned his wings. He was a paratrooper.

He said he did a lot of praying before his first real jump, mostly praying that his parachute would open. He jumped out of C-124 troop carriers, C-119 box carriers, and C-147s. Jumping over the shoreline in Japan worried him the most, because he wasn't a good swimmer. They would jump above the water and had to guide their chute to land on the way down or end up in the water.

His unit was called the Screaming Devils. Dad said they probably called them that because they were all screaming when they jumped out of the planes. Coming back from Japan, they traveled on a troop ship. It took thirteen days to get to the port of Oakland, California. From there he was flown back to Fort Campbell as part of the 101st Airborne Division.

I remember a story he told me once. He met a guy in jump school, a big white guy named Jim. Dad said they became best friends and did everything together wherever they were sent. He said he liked going places with him because it felt like he had his own personal bodyguard. One day in Fort Campbell they went into town for breakfast. They found a breakfast joint and walked in and sat at the counter on the stools, hoping to get a good breakfast. They talked and joked while they were waiting for someone to take their order. A guy with a dirty white apron on walked up and put his hands on the counter and locked his arms and stared at Jim. They both looked his way, thinking he was going to take their order, but he wasn't.

"You are welcome here, but your friend is not," he said, never making eye contact with Dad.

Jim swiveled back and forth on his stool like he was grinding it into the ground, looking the man in the eye. "Can't you see we're both in the service for the same country?" he asked, pointing at Dad's uniform.

The man's scraggly mustache quivered. "That doesn't matter, we're still not serving him."

Jim stood up. "Screw you and your shitty restaurant," he told him, along with a few other choice words. "Let's get out of here, Robert."

Dad walked out of there proud as heck with his buddy Jim.

They left and walked to the next block to a colored restaurant and were welcome and had a down-home breakfast. They got what they wanted: good food.

Up until about fifteen years ago I never really considered the time my parents grew up in. It was a different time, almost another planet as far as I'm concerned. The first time I talked with Dad about it, I was shocked. I didn't know that when he was growing up, like the Blacks he was considered colored and a different class of person. I knew about the prejudice in that time, but I didn't know my parents lived and experienced it firsthand.

I asked Dad, "Why didn't you ever tell me this?"

He just shrugged his shoulders. "It was a long time ago, son."

After that day I asked one of my aunts about it because she grew up in the same period. I was shocked to learn that in little Delano, California, Dad, Mom, my aunt, all of them had to use the colored bathrooms. They had to drink out of the colored faucets, and for some reason, this one shocked me the most. I mean really jolted me. When they went to the movies, the Blacks and the Mexicans had to sit on one side of the theater, and the whites sat on the other side. It still boggles my mind that my parents and family lived through that otherworldly time.

One thing that stands out the most is the answer to the question: why didn't anybody ever tell me about this? The answer was always the same: "That was a long time ago."

My whole life I never heard one of my parents complain about how they were treated. I never heard them say a cross word about white people (I don't even like saying white people, it sounds prejudiced to me). They both had friends of all stripes and never used color as a reference to a person's heart.

In today's world we have people complaining about racism all the time, trying to punish people for crimes against decency that weren't alive at the time it was going on. My dad lived through it but chose to leave it in the past — where it should stay — not to hinder his future, and not to be repeated.

5

His First Love

It was October of 1956. Dad was about to be discharged from the service and was summoned to his commanding officer's office. He walked in the smoke-filled room, happy that he would be headed home soon. His superior was sitting behind his desk, with a twisted spiral of smoke rising from the cigar tucked in the side of his mouth. This is how the conversation went:

"Good morning, Rodriguez," he said, leaning back on his chair.

"Good morning, sir," Dad said, saluting him, not quite sure why he was there.

His superior grinned, probably because he knew Dad was nervous. "At ease, Rodriguez," he said. "I have a proposition for you."

"Yes, sir?"

"I want to offer you a promotion and a pay raise to re-enlist today. What do you think?"

"I'm sorry, sir. I have my heart set on going home."

His superior shuffled some papers in front of him, biting down on the cigar in the corner of his mouth and showing his stained teeth on one side. "What are you going to do when you go home, Rodriguez? Do you have a job waiting for you?"

"I don't, sir."

"Well then, why don't you re-enlist today and get a pay raise and a promotion?"

"I can't, sir," he said, this time keeping it short.

Dad told me the officer pulled the cigar out of his mouth and leaned forward on his chair, sliding his hands toward him on his desk, jutted his chin out, and said, "I hope you have to pick potatoes for the rest of your life and amount to nothing. Get out of my office!"

It didn't faze Dad one bit. He was proud of his service in the military. I personally love the story. I think I've told it more times than he ever did. I laughed with Dad when he first told me and have laughed with the people I've told since then. The funny part is that he did pick potatoes when he came home, but not for life. He left the service with an Honorable Discharge, a Good Conduct Medal, a National Defense Service Medal, an Expert Badge with a Carbine Bar, and a Parachutist Badge.

A few days later he hopped on a Greyhound bus and headed home to Delano. He stayed in a rooming house for men with two of his brothers. The rooms were behind a bar, and the owner, Gonzalo, was also a field contractor. They paid him rent and worked for him in the fields.

Dad told me that when he got out of the service, he basically just goofed around for a while. He wasn't taking life too seriously. But one day something in his life changed. He was walking down the road and noticed some girls sitting on the front porch of a house watching him walk by. His eyes zoomed in on one of them, and their eyes met. She had long reddish-brown hair draped over her shoulders and resting on her lap. He said he had to consciously make himself look away, because he was staring at her, and only her. Something clicked inside him, he just wasn't aware of it yet. He hadn't ever met her, but there was a connection. He kept walking, but he wouldn't forget her.

Some time passed and he was at a dance with one of his brothers, holding up the walls, not dancing, and trying to be cool. He noticed the girl he'd seen in front of the house with her sisters, and she noticed him. The band started and he made that long walk across the dance floor that many guys have made to ask a girl to dance, not knowing whether she would say yes. He knew if she said no it would be an even longer walk back. She said yes, and they danced. Her name was Sara Renteria. I can see him dancing now, he had one move. I called

it the Bean Masher Move. His fists clinched and mashing downward like he was mashing refried beans in a cast-iron skillet with is eyes squinted.

The rest of the evening they danced every song, content with their partner. Before the night was over, he asked her to go on a date to the show. She said yes. From that day forward, they were a couple. They dated for little over a year, until one day she pulled up in her father's car, and he came out to meet her. She was crying.

"What's wrong?" he asked her.

"My dad was drinking, and he started cussing me out for no reason."

Dad was upset but had a solution. Over the past year they had become inseparable, and in Dad's words, "We loved each other so much." The solution was easy. He reached into the car and grabbed her hand. "Marry me," he asked.

She felt the same way about him, and the answer was simple: "Yes."

A few days passed, and he built up enough courage to ask her father for her hand in marriage. It was June 10, 1958, and a real hot day. They wanted to get married in August of that same year. He pulled up to the front of her house, and her dad was in the front yard watching him park with a stern look on his face. Dad said he'd never been that nervous in his whole life. He got out of the car and made the long walk to meet him face to face. Dad asked him how he was doing and got no response, just pursed lips and a low grumble. It wasn't storybook. Dad got right to the point. "I came to ask for Sara's hand in marriage."

Her father looked Dad in the eyes and started pacing back and forth across the front yard. It was an eternity for Dad. He said he paced for at least half an hour, without a word. That's what it seemed like to him, anyway. But the answer finally came: "Yes." Telling me, he said he could still feel the excitement of the day.

On August 30, 1958, they were married in St. Mary's

Church in Delano, California and became husband and wife. It was a small wedding, money was scarce. They were married on Saturday and Dad was back to work on Monday. They rented a small apartment and filled it with second-hand furniture, a modest beginning.

Life moved quick. Sara got pregnant soon after they married, and money got tight. But that didn't matter, they were about to receive a treasure. There's something about having a child that transcends what is normal around us. It's like hearing a song that takes you to another place, one that only that song can accomplish. Dad watched a baby grow, wrapped comfortably in its mother's womb. The baby was part of him. He had all the fears and excitement that run through a parent's mind. But he and his new wife knew a small miracle was on the way. And on May 29, 1959 at 7:52 a.m., they received their treasure. A baby girl: Maria Dolores Rodriguez.

As a father, I can imagine the first time he held her. 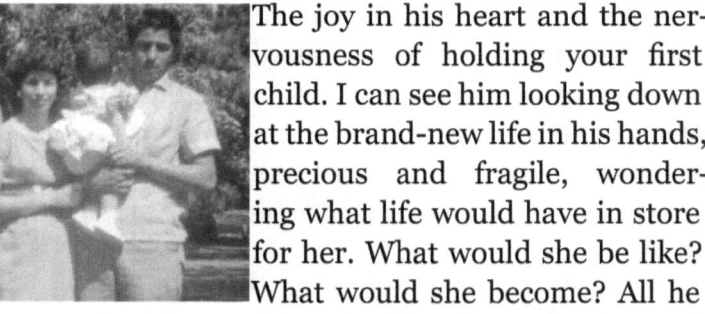 The joy in his heart and the nervousness of holding your first child. I can see him looking down at the brand-new life in his hands, precious and fragile, wondering what life would have in store for her. What would she be like? What would she become? All he knew was that she was his *mija* (daughter), another girl he loved, instantly, with all his heart. They had transcended from husband and wife to what has propelled this world for millennia: they were a family.

6

A New Home

In 1960, Robert and Sara moved from Delano to San Jose, California. They lived with her sister Josie and brother-in-law Juan for three months. Then they bought a brand-new home. I don't have any record of it, but if I remember right, they were able to buy it with a VA loan. It was a small three-bedroom house, perfect for a small family, for an astronomical price: $11,500. I wish we had those prices today.

They moved into their new home and started their new life. Sara became pregnant with her second child, and on May 18, 1961, a new baby boy was born into the Rodriguez family. They named him Roberto Rodriguez, Jr. That's me! That's when I came into the picture. I was blessed and didn't know it yet.

Like most young families, they struggled to make ends meet. But there was no shortage of happiness. They loved each other, and my sister and me, and vowed to each other that they would not put their kids through the things they had to endure growing up. They wanted what makes society better: a better life for their children. They didn't give us everything we wanted, but they gave us the most important things a parent can give: their unconditional love and their faith in God.

It's funny how some of our memories as children are so vivid, never to be forgotten. My earliest memory of my time on this earth is being in church. Crazy, I know. It was a place I would come to know as Most Holy Trinity. I couldn't have been more than two. I remember my sister Mary kneeling next to me with her hands in the prayer position, and Mom and Dad kneeling on either side of us. I was on my back on the kneeler, looking up at them squirming around. I remember Mom reaching down and petting my head like a puppy and smiling at me, and Dad with his arm around Mary. The connection between living on this earth and faith was made with that memory. The importance of it was cemented in my life that day and it would become one I would need to draw on later in life.

Both Dad and Mom had a rough life. They both struggled with their family to survive, and both had fathers that were abusive when drinking. They witnessed and had to endure all the heartache that goes with addiction. But when their firstborn, my sister Mary, came along, they promised each other that life would be different for their children. History tends to repeat itself in families, both good and bad. But they knew it could be different for them if they committed to God and each other. Their goal was for their children to never witness what they had. They didn't necessarily speak those words to each other, but they lived them. Both Mary and I were witnesses to that.

    We did everything together. Every trip included all four of us. We visited family together, we went camping together, we went to church together. It didn't matter where we were, it was the four of us. The fact that they barely scraped by didn't reflect how rich we were as a family.

7

Big Boots

Living in San Jose wasn't easy at first. Mom and Dad struggled. Dad worked at any job he could find to keep us fed and keep life in order at home. Mary and I never felt the pinch of not having enough money; Dad and Mom quietly carried that burden for us. But as most people know, sometimes little kids hear things they weren't intended to hear, or understand, good or bad, and never forget. I don't remember how old I was, but I remember they both still looked big to me. They were standing by the stove in the kitchen. I stood looking up at them not realizing that I would never forget the conversation they were having. My mom walked over to the refrigerator and opened the door, gesturing inside. "All we have are these beans and that little piece of meat."

"I haven't got paid yet, give the kids the meat and we'll just have beans," Dad said.

It wasn't anything earth-shattering, or something that hasn't been done by another parent before, but it was a pattern, a way of thinking, a way of living they chose to follow. Family was everything. We didn't need to hear them say "I love you." We knew it.

Dad eventually found a good job with the City of San Jose. This may sound crazy, but what I remember the most about Dad working for the city, is his boots. I couldn't wait for Dad to come home from work every day. Mom would call out, "Dad's home!" Mary and I would run to the front door to greet the biggest man on earth. "Daddy's home!" It sounds corny, I know, but that's how it was.

We'd open the door to greet him, and there he was, a big dark man with a thick black mustache and a head full of hair the same color. I remember his big smile that revealed the gap between his two front teeth. Bucket seats, he called them. He would squat down to our level and give his two favorite kids in the world a hug of a lifetime. One of the thousands he would give. He would walk over and give his love a kiss on the lips and a hug with a different kind of love, one that only a husband and wife can share, one that has love for their children and for each other wrapped in one.

I would follow him around the house until he took his boots off. It was a routine we had, and he knew what I wanted. He'd pull them off beside his bed and slide them toward me. "There you go, son."

They were size twelve, huge to me. He worked on the road crew patching holes when he first started with the City, so they were covered with dark smudges from the asphalt. I didn't care. I would drop my feet down into the boots and drag them slowly down our hallway to show Mary and Mom that I was just like Dad, until I couldn't drag them anymore.

I'm fifty-nine now, and all these years later I remember those early years and Dad's boots as if it were today. I thank God for giving us the ability to remember and replay a memory that means so much to us, whenever and as many times as we want. It is a gift and a miracle. It's biology too, but more than that. Truly.

I think about it today and realize the significance of those boots. Without saying or knowing it, I was letting myself and the people around me know that I wanted to be like my dad. I wanted to love my wife the way he loved his. I wanted to love my children the way he did, and I wanted to be a good and strong person, one my family could count on, just like him. We've all heard that it's the little things that matter in life. It's true. Sometimes those little things become the big things in our life, and we realize they were part of the foundation laid that made us who we are. I know today that those beat-up size twelve boots were more than just boots. They were one of the many bricks Dad laid to give me the solid foundation I needed to succeed as a person and endure whatever life might throw my way.

8

Groom and Clean

It seemed like the world revolved around our family. I didn't know what that meant back then, but I knew what it felt like. I was living the dream and didn't know it. Every memory I have of San Jose is good. We were a family, and my sister and I experienced what every child should, a connection with family and friends. It taught us without teaching us that family and friends are important, that we all need each other for the good times and the bad, something I would come to learn later in my life. But there was one more constant that stood above everything else and was never compromised: going to church. It didn't matter what was going on, where we were, who we were with, we always made it to church.

They say that our home is our first church. It's true. It's where everything begins for a child. My earliest memories of church started at home. We had two adjoining bathrooms with a pocket door in between. Mom and Mary would be in one, and Dad and me in the other. Dad would lift me onto a little stool in front of the mirror. Mom would do the same with Mary in the other bathroom and start braiding. He would slide the drawer open beside me and pull out a big tube of Groom & Clean. I can still smell it and remember its bluish-green color. He would squirt a pile onto his palm and rub his hands together and slap it onto my head. Even today I can feel his fingers running through my hair as I watched him in the reflection of the mirror, something I would relive later in life. He would whip his little black comb out of his back pocket that had old hair goop nestled in between its teeth and start combing. Dad and I were always ready before Mom and Mary. I can still hear him: "Come on, girls, we're gonna be late."

"We'll be ready, we'll be ready," I'd hear Mom say.

Dad would pace around, warm up the car. "Girls, *vamonos*, let's go," he'd say. "The car is already warmed up."

We'd hear them laugh. "We'll be there. We're almost done."

Somehow, we'd make it to church on time. Dad called it the Sunday miracle.

I remember walking into church looking forward to its end, because that's where the real fun started. And I'm sure every kid in that church had the same sentiment. When the front doors of the church opened and everyone started funneling out, all the kids had one thing on their mind: get to the hall as fast as you can to get your Mexican sweetbread and milk. We'd gobble it down so we could get to the playground across from the hall with all the other kids. Mom and Dad would go to the hall for coffee, sweetbread and fellowship with the other parents while we played. We were all making those much-needed connections to other people.

When I was seven years old, a member of our church, Robert Palacios, started teaching guitar to a group of kids from the church. Dad took Mary and me to every practice. His house was tiny. He crammed twelve kids with guitars into his living room, and somehow, he taught us all to play in church. A miracle in itself. Dad sang with the group, and Mom made the outfits for all the kids. It was a good time in my life that prepared Mary and me for other things. The image of Dad singing by the altar as we played our guitars, I can't forget. His presence meant security, even though I wouldn't understand what it meant until I became a parent myself.

I don't think he realized what he was doing either. He didn't know that being part of everything in my life, was building a man out of a young son. He didn't know that his presence and love would mold me and create a father that would want to take care of and love his own family one day. And he didn't know that his daughter would be subconsciously watching him, watching all of his actions as a father that would make her want a husband with good qualities. He couldn't see or guarantee our future, but he showed us what it could be.

9

Not Just a Car

Dad and Mom called out to Mary and me one Saturday morning, "Get up, kids. We're going to get a new car."

The first thing I thought was, *What about cartoons?* Back then you only had one day to watch cartoons, Saturday morning. Dad sat with me and Mary every week to watch *Wile E. Coyote and the Road Runner, Longhorn Foghorn, Bugs Bunny*, and all those classics that today's cartoons can't hold a candle to. But I was excited about getting a new car, even though I'd have to wait a whole week to watch cartoons again.

As we pulled up to the car lot, Mary and I pointed at different cars. "Is that it? I want that one. Which one are we buying, Dad?"

We walked into the showroom, and the salesman walked up to Mary and me first. "Good morning, kids," he said, handing each of us a sucker. That was enough to make the sale for us. "We have your car ready, Mr. and

Mrs. Rodriguez." I guess they had already made the deal. "Come into my office to sign a few papers and I'll have them bring the car out."

By the time we walked out of his office, a brand new 1966 Plymouth Fury II four-door sedan was parked outside the showroom window. "There she is," the salesman said, pointing.

It was beige with shiny chrome all over it and whitewalls on the tires that highlighted the hubcaps. They brought the keys to Dad. "There's your new car, Mr. Rodriguez."

Dad turned to us. "You kids ready to ride in your new car?" We were already headed that way. We sat in the back bouncing like a couple of Mexican jumping beans. Dad and Mom were just as happy. "Man, this car has power," I remember Dad saying.

We drove around for a while and eventually made our way home. We parked it in our driveway and stood outside looking at it like a big new toy.

"We have another surprise for you," Mom said. Dad looked at her and smiled. "We're going to Disneyland!" You can guess how we reacted.

That was the first family trip in our new car. I remember the excitement that filled the car. It was like four kids going to Disneyland for the first time, not just two. That trip would mark the first of many trips as a family in that car. Short ones, long ones, and always the four of us together.

A vessel is something that transports goods, people, something important to someone. Our Plymouth Fury was not just a car, it was a vessel used by our parents to make memories, to take us to the doctor, to visit family, to go camping, and to go to church in. It was a place where Mary and I played, picked on each other, slept, laughed, and shared times we'd never forget. It was one more way to seal the bond between two parents and their children. It was a thing that was made into something greater than intended: a family vessel.

10

In a Prominent Place

It was December of 1972, and my Tia Josie, my mom's sister, moved to Lindsay, California to open a small store. They were inseparable and did everything together. So, as Tia Josie went, we went too. By 1973 we were making the same move. We sold our house and bought a nice little house in Lindsay for $5,900. Can you imagine getting a house for that price?

Dad's first job was a temporary one with the City of Lindsay. He was a trash collector. It didn't matter to him what he did, as long as it kept his family on their feet.

He was dumping trash one day and saw the edge of a picture frame sticking out above the trash. He put the can back down and pulled it out. He knew it was a picture but couldn't see the image. He pulled his hanky out of his back pocket and glided it lightly across the glass, slowly revealing the picture.

He said he stood looking down at it, because it was in such an odd place to find something like that. He said he looked up toward the house that the trashcan belonged to and wondered why, or how, someone could throw away a picture like the one he held in his hands.

Later that day, I heard our German Shepherd Chano bark, signaling Dad was home from work. Mom was cooking dinner in the kitchen. I heard the front door open. "Look what I found in the trash today," I heard Dad call out.

I was in my room, probably not cleaning it. But I could hear Mom. "That's beautiful. That was in the trash?" she questioned, with disbelief in her voice.

I heard the sound of the beads hanging in Mary's doorway; she was already on her way to see what Dad had found.

"What is it?" Mary asked, as I walked up behind her.

Mom stuck it out in her hands toward us. "It's a picture of Jesus."

I thought it was a nice picture, but I was hoping it might be something cool that I could play with or use for something. I'm sure Mary probably thought the same thing.

Mom cleaned it up and hung it on the wall in the dining room. You couldn't miss it. Every time we walked in the front door, we saw Him; every time we sat down to have dinner, He was in the midst of us. Part of the uniqueness of the picture was that it didn't matter where you were in the room, it looked like His eyes followed you.

Every single person that ever came to our house and saw the picture, commented how beautiful it was. All our friends and family knew the story behind the picture. It seemed to make it more special. It was more than a conversation piece. It was part of the family and it had meaning.

In San Jose, Mom and Dad did their best to keep Jesus in our lives, to let us know that it was important to believe in something greater than ourselves. They didn't preach to us or sit us down and read the Bible to us every night. They didn't have to. Their lives reflected what was inside. Mary and I knew where Jesus stood in our home.

When we moved from San Jose and Dad found the picture of Jesus in the trash and Mom put it on the wall in the dining room, it was a physical representation of where Jesus should be in our lives: in a prominent place.

But sadly, there would be a time when I would take that picture of Jesus down from where it hung in my life, and I would end up doing what the first owner did. I would metaphorically put him in the trash. I would choose to walk by him every day and ignore him, as if He weren't there.

11

M.A.Y.O.

Mary and I made friends right away. Mom and Dad got involved in the church community and started building relationships with other parents, who would become lifelong friends. We went from one good life in San Jose to another in Lindsay. My only complaint was the heat. I couldn't believe how hot it gets in summer in the Central Valley. I got used to it though.

Dad eventually got a good job at a place called Olson Mirrors in Strathmore, California, a small town about five miles from Lindsay. It paid well and he liked it, but not long after he got the job, the company decided to move to another state. Dad was back out on the job hunt. He went out looking every day, but there was one thing I remember that still makes me laugh. He would make sure that his job interviews weren't between 12 and 1 p.m. because he got hooked on a soap opera, *One Life to Live*. From 12 to 1 p.m. he was glued to the TV. One day I walked in and he was sitting pointing at the TV. "Who in the heck is this guy?" he said.

"What?" I said.

"I don't know who this new guy is on the show. Where in the heck did he come from?"

"I don't know, Dad, but I think that's a commercial."

He just laughed.

He found the job he was looking for with the City of Lindsay and would later become Public Works Supervisor. He loved his job and the people he worked with. Mom got a job with the Lindsay Coordinating Council, a place that helped people down on their luck who needed things like food, shelter, and clothing.

Within a year or two Mom and Dad started a youth group for teenagers. They named it M.A.Y.O. (Mexican American Youth Organization). I don't think it was Dad's idea. His mind wasn't geared that way; he didn't go around looking for things to do for other people or ways to make society better. He was good to everyone but didn't go out of his way to volunteer for things. But that's okay, he had someone to do it for him: Mom. She always had something in the works, and Dad willingly followed.

They started the group to help kids stay out of trouble and hopefully help them become good citizens and productive members of our community. And I'm sure they wanted it to be a place where kids could just have fun too.

I loved the group because I got to be around older kids. I thought I was cool, but I was more like the mascot. I remember a girl named Nena gave me a nickname: Chicharrón (which means deep fried pork fat). I don't know why she called me that, but I liked it.

The meetings were fun, and Dad and Mom always had some sort of positive message for us to take home about life. They got us involved in the community and fundraisers so the group could do things together. They arranged carwashes with the local police so the kids could get to know them and see them as friends and not the enemy.

One thing that Mom stressed was doing things for other people for no reason other than to do something good. I didn't understand it then, but I do now. It's one of the greatest human traits: charity for others. An elderly lady named Maybell lived on the corner of our block. She didn't get around too well. Dad offered to have the group come and clean her house and yard. She accepted. He talked to all the kids, and they were excited to do something like that. Dad arranged it for the next Saturday, and about twelve kids showed up early ready to go.

Dad ran the outside crew, and Mom guided the inside. It was a lot of fun, and we all felt good about doing something for someone else. I remember she thanked all of us when we finished. She was grateful. We walked three houses down the road to our house and sat on the front lawn. Mom brought out a bunch of burritos she made, and we ate and laughed, feeling good about what we did. It was one of those days you never forget.

The next day, Sunday, the doorbell rang at about 7:30 in the morning. We were up already getting ready for church. Mom said, "I got it." Mary and I were already headed for the door too. Mom opened the door, and it was Maybell. "Good morning," Mom said.

The first words out of her mouth were, "They stole twenty dollars out of my purse."

Mom's whole body went limp. "Are you sure?" she said, with a shaky voice, like the ground moved beneath her.

Writing this right now, I can feel how she felt, like, *I'm in trouble.* As a parent you have high hopes for your children and when they fail, it hurts. You never want to hear someone say something negative about your son or daughter. Mom and Dad thought of all the girls and boys in the group as sons and daughters. They cared about them.

"Yes, I searched my purse, and it's gone," she said.

By that time Dad was standing behind us at the door.

"Can I go with you to your house to help you look for it, just in case it was misplaced?" Mom asked.

"You can, but I know where I put it."

Mom went with her and we waited. I remember seeing Dad shake his head with his lips crimped a few times, maybe wondering if having the group was worth it. We waited, and Mom came home after about an hour. Dad sat at the kitchen table the whole time, waiting. Mary and I were milling around wanting to know if she found the money. It was only twenty dollars, but it was a lot more than that, it was the group's image.

"We couldn't find it," she said. "We have to call all the kids and have them come over."

Dad just nodded.

If I were Mom or Dad in that situation, I could hear myself telling my wife, "It's probably not worth having this group, I don't need these kinds of problems," or something to that effect. But neither Mary nor I ever heard those sentiments come out of Mom or Dad's mouth.

Mom called all the kids and asked if they could come to the house that afternoon. They arrived one by one, probably wondering why we were having a meeting. When everyone showed up, Mom told them what happened and they all looked instinctively at the person beside them. There was a chorus of the words: "It wasn't me." It was the last thing on their minds when they were called to come over that day.

"If everyone says it wasn't them, we all need to go as a group and apologize to Maybell and give her twenty dollars from our fundraiser money," Mom said.

Everyone looked solemn, and no one jumped up and said, "I did it. I'm sorry."

So we walked over, twelve kids, Mom, and Dad. We knocked on Maybell's door, and it opened. She looked a little shocked to see us standing at her doorstep. One by one each kid apologized for the missing money, including Mom, Dad, Mary, and me. She accepted our apology and the group moved on. I never heard Mom or Dad say a negative word about the group.

A couple of weeks later, there was a knock on our front door at dinner time. "I'll get it." Both Mary and I went to the front door. It was Maybell. Her eyes were watery.

"Can I speak to your mom and dad?" she asked.

By that time they were at the door. "Hi, Maybell," they said.

Tears started rolling down her cheeks. "I'm so sorry. I'm so sorry I accused your group of stealing from me. I grabbed a cup off a shelf today, and the twenty dollars was in there. I forgot I had put it there for safekeeping. I am so sorry."

Mom and Dad smiled. All the hurt they probably felt was instantly relieved. The group's image was restored with an apology. Mom called all the kids and asked if they could meet at our regular meeting place, the Salt Cellar, beneath City Hall. She told them it was a special meeting. I'm sure some of them might have thought, *What now?*

Dad and Mom brought the meeting to order, except this time they had smiles on their faces. "She found the money, she found the twenty dollars!" they said, like it was a million. All the kids were just as excited.

"I want to tell you kids something," Dad said. "I want to tell you that Sara and I are so proud of you. Each one of you was accused of doing something you didn't do. And each one of you were still willing to apologize as individuals and as a group. That's character, and that's a good example of what a family is: no matter what, they stick together. (I can't say those were his exact words, but I know it was the sentiment he conveyed.)

"We have a surprise for you," Mom said. "We're all going camping together."

We went to Camp Nelson, above Springville, California. It was a great time. They had a built-in swimming pool that Mom and Dad rented for a day, just for the group. We all had a blast that week. I know every kid in that group never forgot that trip, and I'm sure they never forgot the lesson they learned about sticking together. I didn't.

12

Commitment

If someone were to ask you what your definition of a father was, could you give them a clear answer? Could you say, "This is exactly what a father should be." I think we could come up with lots of different answers to that question. Every family is different, every family comes from different roots and backgrounds, and every family has a suitcase or two that they would rather not be carrying.

Both Dad and Mom had abusive fathers that were mean when drinking. They both had to witness their mothers being abused and hit sometimes. When his father drank, Dad had to hide for fear of his life because his father considered him defective. That alone could fill a suitcase.

There is no mold, there is no book you can buy that can give you all the answers you need to have a good marriage and raise kids. There is no exact way. Each new couple needs to figure out what they want for their family. As soon as we marry, and as soon as we start having children, we are peppered with decisions. What kind of family do we want to be, how do we want to raise our kids? I don't think a couple sits down and fills out a questionnaire, but some married couples make clear, conscious decisions and commit to them.

I don't know whose idea it was, but when Mary and I were born, they vowed not to pass on their family baggage. I know this because I never witnessed any of the things they suffered in their lives in mine. They remembered everything that happened to them in the past, but never let it become a part of their family's future. They broke the cycle that could have plagued generations. Imagine if all couples could do that today, the world would be a better place.

Mom always said the simple accomplish the greatest things. We can interpret those words in a lot of different ways, but for now, I think of Dad. He wasn't a college graduate and didn't come from a highfalutin background — you know that by now. He was just one of the billions that have walked this earth, but to Mary and me, he was a lot more.

He made the decision early on in his marriage — first, to be there — and then (not to be snarky) to be there. He made a conscious decision, what I consider the most important decision he could have ever made as a husband and a father. He first made a commitment to his wife. Then he made one to Mary and me when we were born. I'm sure he didn't say, "Sara, I commit to you," or "Mary, Robert, I commit to you." But Mary and I would come to understand the meaning of commitment before we knew the word.

As a husband and a father for thirty years I've come to realize that the word commitment is not just a word. It's more than that. It's the most important word in a marriage, and the most important concept a parent can hold in their heart for their children.

When we meet someone and fall in love, we're all gaga (if that's a word) for them and inseparable. We can't wait till the next time we see them. The only decision we have to make is where are we going the next time we see them. It's easy. Then we marry, and decisions start falling from the sky out of nowhere. We need more money, we're barely making it. How can we afford another kid? How are we going to raise them? All the mushy goo goo gaga love disappears without our knowledge. But you keep going, you manage to pay the bills and take care of your children. The fear of tomorrow that percolates to the surface sometimes, you've learned to squash and keep going, no matter what the resistance inside you says. You come home every day and you do your best to let tomorrow worry about tomorrow.

I mentioned that commitment is more than just a word. Its definition in the dictionary doesn't do it justice. It's not complete. Commitment to your wife or husband and to your children is the love that holds your marriage together, even in times of trial. It's the love that bonds you to your children that instills a desire in them to have that same commitment in their own lives.

I didn't learn that on my own, and I didn't hear it come out of Mom and Dad's mouths. I saw it. I watched them treat each other with respect. I listened to the tones they used when they talked to each other, and I learned that love itself cannot sustain a marriage. The letters L-O-V-E are just letters. They're not enough. It's commitment that bonds those four letters together and makes them into a word that has meaning. Action is proof. It doesn't matter what we say, but what we do. Dad and Mom proved to Mary and me through example what love really is: commitment.

13

A Parent's Worst Nightmare

It was a Saturday morning, a perfect day. I had just bought a new dirt bike from a coworker. I wanted to take it out on its first ride. I remember Dad asking me what I was doing up so early. It wasn't normal for me to get up early if I wasn't working. "I'm taking my new motorcycle out for a ride," I said, pointing at it.

He nodded. "Be careful."

Be careful? What does that mean to a twenty-year-old that thinks they're indestructible and has never seen or considered death? Those words never came out of my mouth, but I'm sure I subconsciously thought it. At that age you only see life and what's on your list to do next, not its end.

I got ready and went outside and gassed up my new bike. Mom slid the kitchen window open. "You going to eat breakfast?"

"Naw, I'm not hungry," I told her. The thought of flying down the road in a few minutes was enough to fill my stomach.

"Where's your helmet?"

"I'm just going right here," I said, pointing toward the orange grove just past our street.

I sat on the bike by the curb in front of our house, contemplating the power beneath me, craving the feeling of all the torque the motor had in store for me. I looked toward the house, and Dad and Mom were sitting at the kitchen table looking my way. I waved and they waved back at me and smiled. I stood up and put my foot on the kick-start and thrust downward, bringing the bike to life. It rumbled and popped just like a dirt bike should. I revved it up and popped the clutch separating the front tire from the road beneath it. It only took about thirty seconds for me to be on a country road, our house was the last block on our side of town. From there orange groves covered the landscape.

I've written about this day before, but only from my perspective. Until this day, I've only considered my side of the story. There were a lot of other people that were an important part of it. Here's what happened.

The air was crisp. My long hair flapped in my face as I zipped down the road with no helmet for protection. I made it to Strathmore Road. It runs along the edge of the foothills and the Friant canal system that supplies water to farmers in the Central Valley.

Flying down the road, I noticed two men pruning trees on the edge of the road. They were looking my way and probably heard me coming from a mile away. They were both on ladders watching me as I flew by. Down about a quarter mile from them there was a dirt drive leading up to the canal bridge and up into the foothills.

A perfect place for a good ride on a dirt bike. I turned onto it and barreled up toward the bridge. I glanced at the water as I passed. I turned back, but it was too late. A metal cable tied across the dirt drive was already sliding up the handlebars and headed toward me, with no time to flinch or squeeze the brakes. The cable caught me in the neck and flung me back in the opposite direction.

Meanwhile, Dad and Mom were getting ready to go to Delano. They had no idea their son was lying clotheslined by a cable on a dirt drive where no one could see him. They were headed to an event for the Cursillo, a group that has three-day retreats for couples and singles at church. It was a normal day for them.

As a parent of two grown kids, I understand what it is to worry about your kids. You never stop. Even if you aren't thinking of them at any given moment, you always want to know they're safe. At that moment I was lying on that dirt drive, Mom and Dad thought their son was okay, just as they'd last seen him that morning.

I somehow managed to get up from the ground. I couldn't turn my head, my neck swelled tight like a balloon. I wasn't breathing through my mouth. I had a hole in my neck that was somehow allowing me to breathe and stay on my feet. I only had one thing on my mind: stay alive. I pleaded, not in words, but in thought: *Please don't let me die, Lord.* Over and over I said those words. It's funny where we turn to when we don't see the light at the end of the tunnel, but only the end of the road.

Dad and Mom were probably giving a talk to the candidates that were attending the retreat, or just helping in the kitchen. They didn't care what they were asked to do, they just wanted to be part of the success of the retreat. Retreats and meetings were a normal part of their lives. Mary and I were always a part of it too, because they always brought us along when we were kids; all the parents brought their kids. They would have their meetings in the church hall or one of the rooms, and all of us kids were outside running around playing games, doing what kids do.

I lifted my arms and they were covered with blood. I told myself: "Put them down! Don't look at them or you'll never make it." I put them down and started walking across the canal bridge and down the hill toward the paved road. I made it back down to Strathmore Road and started walking on the yellow line hoping someone would see me. God heard my plea. The same two guys I'd passed a few minutes earlier saw me. I must have looked like a zombie covered in blood breathing through my neck. I don't remember anything they said on the way to the hospital, but I'm sure they were thinking: "Man, this guy is jacked up."

We made it to the local hospital, and the two men walked me into the emergency room, then disappeared. A layer of skin around my neck was gone. When I hit the cable, I must have rolled on it before it slung me back in the opposite direction. Two different doctors came in to look at me at different times. They both asked me if I had been choked. I could only motion with my hands that I was on a motorcycle and hit something. They left me alone in the room, almost as if they didn't know what to do.

After about forty-five minutes had passed, Mary walked in. I had been alone for most of that time, breathing through my neck. "What happened?" she asked.

I motioned like I did for the doctors.

"What have they done for you?"

I motioned with my finger: nothing.

"I'll be right back," she said, walking out of the room.

Growing up, Mary was always a foot taller than me. She tormented me, picked on me, and harassed me like brothers and sisters do. But she was also my protector, my big sister that always looked after me. She always knew what to do. And I knew if Mom and Dad weren't around, I could always count on her.

She walked back in with one of the doctors. He walked up and touched my neck. "Are you sure you weren't choked?" he asked again.

I motioned again with my hands. It was a motorcycle accident.

"Hmm," is all he said.

Mary walked up close. "I want you to send him to Kaweah Delta Hospital in Visalia." It wasn't a request, and the doctor knew it. He complied. Within five minutes they were loading me into the ambulance.

In 1981 there were no cell phones, no email, and no personal computers. They were still in someone's imagination. Either you were sitting near a landline or you didn't get the call. Mom and Dad were an hour away, with no way of knowing what was going on. But somehow, they got the message.

It's a parent's worst nightmare to hear that their son or daughter was in a bad accident. I've always told this story only from my perspective. I never considered what they might have felt that day. I think about the moment they got the news. I can see someone walking up to Mom and whispering in her ear: "Your son was in a bad accident."

I can feel her heart drop, and I can see their faces in disbelief. I think about them driving from Delano to Visalia, hoping they would find their son alive. No parent wants to travel that road. I can see Dad driving, holding Mom's hand, telling her, "He's going to be okay," and looking her way, while Mom nodded with tears pulsing down her cheeks.

They unloaded me and wheeled me into the emergency room. A doctor came right in and pressed his fingers on different parts of my neck. He looked up toward a nurse. "Wheel him into the next room," he said.

Mary was standing beside me making sure they took care of her little brother. She was born to care for sick people. That was her gift.

I don't think it was the operating room, but within a matter of seconds doctors surrounded me. "We're going to give you a little shot," one said. The nurse brought a tray with different tools on it. He grabbed a scalpel. "We're going to help you breathe a little better, okay?" I blinked. That's all I could do. After he made his cut, he grabbed some forceps and stuck them in my neck and pulled my windpipe out. I had severed it in half. I could hear flapping. He put a tube in it so it wouldn't collapse, and I could breathe. It felt so good. "Prep him for surgery," the doctor said.

We have someone who wants to see you before you go into surgery, Robert," one of the nurses said. I was so happy. It was Mom and Dad. Somehow, they made it. We were together like we had always been. All the doctors in the world couldn't have given me as much comfort as knowing the family that loved me was there.

Dad and Mom put their hands on my chest, and Mary put hers on my shoulder. They were all smiling down at me. I can't imagine what they were thinking at the time, seeing their son and brother with his neck opened. "You're going to be okay. We love you and we'll see you when you get out of surgery," they told me.

I still remember Dad giving a smile of reassurance before they wheeled me off. He said everything I needed to hear, without saying a word.

The next thing I remember was waking up for a little bit after surgery in intensive care and hearing: "Come on! Come on! You can do it! Come on! Fight! Don't give up!"

I woke up three days later and was told that there was another young boy my age that was in a bad motorcycle accident too but didn't make it. Dad told me the parents were crushed. It was another family that had suffered the worst fate. Ours was spared.

When I got home my mom had a decoupage picture she had made on a grape tray for a wall in my room. I still have it on the wall in my office. It's a beautiful picture of Jesus's hands. On the back she wrote: "Son, on February 21, 1981, the Lord held you in his hands and blessed us by giving you back to us. We love him for his gift, and you for being our son."

We were a complete family. They still had me, and I still had them. Dad and Mom had avoided a parent's worst nightmare: the loss of a child. But we had a future not lived yet, one that held a different outcome.

14

The Seeds We Plant

The difference between Mary and me was one of us had drive, and the latter only wanted to drive. As soon as I got my license, it was all about me. What was I going to do next? What new thing could I get for my car that would make more girls like me? Even though that doesn't work, at least for the nice ones. But, I thought it did at the time.

I stopped going to church because I was too cool, and too busy, or so I thought. I'll be honest, I was a selfish, self-serving jerk, and an idiot too. But I didn't care. Years later I talked to Mom and Dad about not going to church, and they told me it killed them when I stopped going. They said they went and talked to Fr. Leitheiser, our parish priest, and asked him what they should do. His answer was short: "Nothing. You did your job and you've taught him the best you could. The choice is his now. Pray for him, but he has to find his own way."

They learned, like every parent, that there's no guarantee that what we pray for and want for our children, they will want for themselves. This I know.

Fr. Leitheiser was right: I did have to find my own way back. It took a while. I got my license in 1977, and it would be eleven years before I came to my senses. I'm glad Mom and Dad kept praying.

I was asked to be in a friend's wedding. I didn't know who my partner was, but they told me she was cute. That's all I knew. At the first rehearsal, we were all lined up ready to start and she was late — the story of her life. She walked up next to me. She had long brown wavy hair and dark eyes, like black pearls. Cristy was her name. She was wearing Wrangler jeans and cowboy boots and had a wad of chewing gum in her mouth. She was a cowgirl, horse and all. What a combination — I was a lowrider. Before we went into the church, Fr. Leitheiser said there was no chewing gum in church. She pulled it out of her mouth and stuck it to her boot and laughed. So, guess what I figured out? She was just as nutty as me.

It didn't take long for us to fall for each other. About three weeks after we met, Mom and Dad poked their head through my bedroom door one Saturday morning and told me, "We can tell you like this girl and are having a lot of fun."

I guess it was a dead giveaway when they heard me, a lowrider, blasting country music from my car stereo. "Yeah, I do like her," I said.

They nodded. "We're happy for you, son."

I know as a parent now that one of the most important things you hope for is that your kids are safe and happy.

Six weeks after we met, I proposed to her, and within

two months we were married. Our parents were so happy. I don't know what made them happier, the fact that we had found each other, or that they were finally going to get us out of their houses.

Cristy and I coming together brought many blessings to the family. Parents don't always get to see the fruits of their labor when raising kids, they just have to trust that they're doing the right thing and making the right choices. There was one blessing that made Mom and Dad happiest of all: when I met Cristy and realized she was more than just a date, or a girlfriend, something deep inside me clicked. The seed they had planted in my earliest memories that had died, sprouted and came back to life. The desire to bring God back into my life, and into the family I might have, burned inside me. I can almost touch the feeling I had back then writing about it. It's real. Everything they said, everything they did, and everything they lived, proved to be fruitful. Their son came home.

I wanted the same thing they wanted for Mary and me, for mine. To know that there is something greater than us out there; something that holds everything together; something that can guide you when the undertow in life drags you far out to sea. For this above everything, I am grateful. I would have to draw on that wisdom to navigate the treacherous waters life had planned for me.

15

Simon of Cyrene

The years passed. Cristy and I had a son, Robert Michael, and a daughter, Sara Cristina, named after Mom. Happy is the best way to describe our life. Mary had three children: a daughter, Eva Marie, and two boys, Louie Benito and Vicente Carlos. Dad and Mom were retired, enjoying life and their grandchildren. They were close with my in-laws, Mike and Maria. They went on cruises together and road trips to Baja. It was a perfect picture.

In August of 1999, Cristy and I had a trip planned to Lake Mead in Arizona. We would leave on August 21st for a week-long vacation there. Even our Plymouth Voyager van seemed excited about going. We were venturing out farther and farther with each trip we took.

While we were just about ready to go on our trip, Mary and her family were on their way back from one of their own. They were on a two-week trip to visit family and sightsee in Mexico. But they had an extra passenger: Mom. They would be home on August 20, and we were leaving the next day.

When Mom and Dad retired, I would go to their house every day to spend a little time with them. They loved having their son over, and I loved being there. A couple of days before they left on their trip to Mexico, I was visiting them on my lunch, and Dad asked Mom: "Do you have to go?"

Dad and I were sitting in the living room, and Mom was leaning on the doorway going into the hall. "I have to," she said. "I have to go."

I remember Dad crimping his lips. "Okay," he said, wishing she had given him a different answer. Dad wasn't used to her not being around.

The day before Mary and the family went on their trip, she was driving home from work in Visalia, where she was a nursing instructor for a local college. I was home and my cell phone rang: "Hello?"

"Hi, what are you doing?"

It was Mary. I could hear a lot of background noise. She was in her van that flew from place to place. "Nothing, just here with Cristy and the kids. How are you, sis?"

"Just headed home to make sure we're ready for the trip and to see if the kids did what I asked them to do," she laughed.

I laughed too. I knew what she meant.

Mary was always go go go. That's the best way to describe her.

"I'm trying to use all the minutes I have left on my phone, I don't want to lose them," she said.

In 1999 cell phones were just coming out, and everything was regulated by minutes, depending on your plan. If you went over your minutes, they charged you extra. I mean up the wazoo. And if you didn't use them all, you lost them.

I talked with her until she pulled into her driveway. "I'm home," she said.

"Do you think the kids did everything you asked them to do?" I asked her.

"Heck no, they're running around in the front yard. I'll call you later."

I laughed. "Okay, I'll be by in the morning to see you before you leave."

I broke away from work the next morning and stopped by Mom and Dad's place to tell Mom bye. We talked for a few minutes. We hugged. "I love you, Mom. I'll see you when you get back," I told her.

"*Sí Dios permite* (If God permits)," she said. She always said that, and I was about to find out why.

I headed over to Mary's place to tell the family bye. I pulled up to their house, and the front door was open. There were suitcases, jackets, and everything else they were taking on the trip piled on the hardwood floor inside the doorway. Mary poked her head out, rolling her eyes at me. I laughed, because I knew everything wasn't going as planned. We talked for a few minutes while she was trying to get the kids to do what she asked.

"I better get back to work," I told her. I told my brother-in-law Louie bye, and gave the kids a hug. I gave Mary a big goodbye hug on their porch and told her I loved her, and she did the same. She followed me down the steps to the front gate and closed it behind me. I turned around to tell her I loved her again and had the urge to open the gate and go back in and give her another hug, but I didn't. I wish I had. I hopped into my work truck and waved. "I love you, sis. Have fun."

She smiled and waved. "Love you too."

Two weeks passed, and it was Friday, August 20. Mary, Mom, and the family were coming home. They would be back early, they said. I was excited about seeing them before we left on our trip the next day. I missed them. I went to work that morning like usual. I worked for an irrigation district. I still do. We deliver water to the farmers in our community. I was on my morning route and stopped at our pumping plant in front of the gate and got out, leaving my truck door open. I headed toward the gate to unlock it. "Car seven," I heard come out of our old Motorola two-way radio. I kept walking toward the gate "Car seven!" the voice said with more force, like it was important.

It was our dispatcher, Bill. I thought he was going to make a change on someone's water order. I reached into the truck and picked up the mic and stretched the cord outside where I was standing. "Go ahead, Bill."

"Robert, you need to get home."

"What's going on, Bill?"

"Robert, please get home, you need to get home," he pressed.

"Okay, Bill," is all I said. I knew then something was wrong. It was a seven-minute drive home from Strathmore. I prayed all the way there that nothing had happened to one of my kids. All the way home, *Please don't let it be anything bad*, I thought over and over. But I knew I was going home to something terrible.

We live on the outskirts of town by the foothills of the Sierra Mountains. As I turned down our road, I could see my aunt Josie's red Camry parked in front of our house. I remember as I parked across the street, Cristy and Tia Josie stood outside the front gate. Cristy's eyes were tearing, she looked helpless. Tia Josie had a blank look on her face, and Dad was sitting in the passenger's seat with a pasty look I had never seen before.

"What's going on?" I asked.

Dad got out of the car with a shattered look. "They were in a bad accident," he said, forcing the words out of his mouth.

"What happened, where are they now?"

"Some are in Delano, and some are in Bakersfield," Tia Josie said.

By that time Cristy had her arm around me, with tears rolling down her cheeks, "I'm sorry, Robert, I'm so sorry," she said.

"We need to go," Tia said.

"Is everyone okay?" I asked.

"Mary," Dad said, shaking his head.

I gave no reply. I was as numb as everyone else. Cristy squeezed me, trying to convey some sort of comfort that words couldn't deliver.

"We have to go," Tia said again.

Cristy stayed, to get the kids ready to go to the hospital.

Tia Josie drove, Dad sat in the passenger seat, and I sat in the back. It was a weird drive to Delano, about forty minutes from Lindsay. The conversation was small. No one in the car knew what to say. What do you say in a situation like that? What is there to talk about? What words can change a situation you know nothing about? There are none.

Going through life we hear about somebody dying in a car accident in someone else's family that we know. We say, "That's terrible. I feel so bad for them," and we mean it. But we really don't understand because the death isn't at our doorstep. It's at a distance. The real pain of the loss doesn't cut into our heart. But as anyone who has lived on this earth for any amount of time knows, it's impossible to get through this life with a heart that is unscathed. On August 20, 1999, it was our turn to experience the worst life had to offer.

We walked in the front doors of Delano District Hospital and were greeted by my cousin Ray, Tia Josie's son. Not thirty seconds later a representative came and introduced himself and walked us to a room where we could talk. My body was stiff from head to toe. Dad had the look of a sheep headed for slaughter.

"The first thing I want you to know is that Beni, Vicente, and Louie are going to be okay. They're all hurt and need to stay in the hospital, but their injuries are not life-threatening," he said.

It was a relief to hear that, but I knew the bomb hadn't dropped yet.

The representative put his hands on his hips and drooped his head. "But I'm sorry to say, Mary didn't make it."

Dad just nodded his head slowly with his eyes closed.

"We don't know how Sara and Eva are doing, they were rushed to Bakersfield. But you need to get there quick," he said.

My cousin Ray drove us to the hospital. By the time we got there, Mom had passed. They were trying to stabilize Eva, who had massive internal injuries, for surgery. Things are a little blurry, but I remember a gentleman came and got Dad and me. We followed him to the elevator and went down a few flights. The doors opened and we stepped out into a quiet hallway. We followed him. I knew where we were headed — to see Mom like we never intended to.

The man stopped at an extra-wide door. He turned and looked at us with deer eyes. "I'm really sorry," he said as he opened the door.

It was a tiny room, just long enough for the gurney Mom was lying on, and room for maybe three to four people to stand in. We walked in and stood beside her.

"I'll give you some time alone with her. I'm really sorry about your loss," he said as he closed the door.

Mom looked just like herself, somehow the accident had spared her face. I'm glad, because even though it was a dreadful scene, Mom's face was as I had always known it.

We stood looking down at her. The once vibrant, full of life, full of love mother, wife, grandmother, sister, and friend lay there silent with only the memories of her life remaining. Her clock had stopped, her life had ended. As the Bible says, "Like a thief in the night, at an hour unbeknownst to us, death will come."

It's funny how after losing someone, you replay the things they said before they passed, and it almost seems like they knew. We later learned that on the day of the accident, just after it happened, some girls stopped to help. They were nursing students headed to Cal State Bakersfield, where Mary got her nursing degree and her master's. They said that Mom kept saying: *"My Mija, my Mija* (My daughter, my daughter.)"

Thinking about Dad and me standing next to Mom lying still, reminds me of the day before they left on their trip and Dad asked her, "Do you have to go?"

And she said, "I have to."

As a parent I've always said if one of my kids were to die before me, I would feel like I had to go with them, to protect them. I think about Mom saying, "I have to go." And her saying, "*My Mija, my Mija,*" while she was still alive. I see clearly now why she had to.

Earlier in this chapter I mentioned that Mary called me the day before they left on their trip on her way home from work on her cell phone. If you remember, I mentioned that in 1999 everything on cell phones was regulated by minutes. You only had so many each month on your plan, and if you didn't use them, you lost them. I remember Mary clearly saying to me, "I still have minutes left on my phone and I don't want to lose them."

Today I see those words as her saying, "My time is short, brother, and I want to spend what I have left talking to you." What both Mom and Mary said before the accident means the world to me.

There was a knock on the door. I reached back and opened it. It was Fr. Alex, our parish priest in Lindsay. He's a small man, maybe five feet if he's lucky. He walked straight over to Mom and put his hand on her forehead and said a prayer. I don't remember the words, but the image of his hand on her forehead and Mom lying still receiving his blessing is etched in my heart. He turned to us and said, "You know it's not over."

We agreed and talked for a few minutes and there

was another knock on the door. It was the man who brought us to the room. "We need you to come up to surgery, they're about to take Eva in."

We followed at a fast pace into the elevator and up a few floors. He ushered us to the big surgery doors. Everything was hurried. All the family was there, they were letting everybody see her before she went into surgery. That wasn't a good sign, that meant she had a multitude of internal injuries, and that she might not make it through surgery. They walked Dad and me through the crowd of family there to where Eva was. Doctors and nurses were all around her, we knew we had to be quick. She was awake with her eyes wide open and a tube down her throat. Both Dad and I latched onto her hand. "You're going to be okay," we told her. "We love you. We'll all be waiting for you when you get out," I told her. But it was a lie. It wasn't true, everyone wouldn't be waiting for her when she came out. Her mom and grandma couldn't be there. The two people she needed the most, were gone.

She wiggled her head, with fear in her eyes.

Dad and I came back out into the large waiting room. It was full of family and friends coming over crying and hugging us. I remember looking over toward Dad, six-two, a strong man crushed by life trying to hold his composure.

Eva was in surgery. My two nephews and my brother-in-law were in Delano, but they might as well have been a million miles away. Earlier that day they were a family, complete and together. They were asleep, almost home, dreaming about their next adventure as a family. Mom, I'm sure, couldn't wait to see her honey, her love who completed who she was, standing on the front steps of their house smiling and happy she was home. But that didn't happen. The winds of life changed, and it was in the form of a van and a reckless driver. And those that woke weren't dreaming of their next adventure anymore, they were living a nightmare they couldn't wake up from.

Eva came out of surgery and was stable, which gave us something to be thankful for. We had something to smile about that day.

Family members made sure that my two nephews and my brother-in-law had plenty of visitors in Delano, where they were in the hospital. Writing this makes me feel sick to my stomach, because I never broke away when they were in the hospital. Beni was thirteen — a confusing time already made a million times worse. And Vicente, ten years old, was just a baby himself. I know lots of family were letting them know they were loved, but I wasn't. It kills me today to think I wasn't there, they were living the same nightmare the rest of us were, but worse, their Mom was gone.

Eva's survival was the bright spot in our darkness. I stayed with her twenty-four hours a day, because her dad and her brothers couldn't be there. I couldn't leave. She was fifteen, about to turn sixteen. Her mom couldn't be there to give her the strength she needed to get through this awful time. It was the worst scenario, a family broken apart, never to be the same.

My brother-in-law Michael, Cristy's brother, came up to me in the waiting room the day of the accident and hugged me and told me he loved me, something he doesn't do on a regular basis. It's weird, out of all the conversations I had that day, I remember the one I had with him the most. He told me, "As we drove from Lindsay to Bakersfield, I noticed all the people in their cars, they were oblivious to the tragedy we're living right now. It's as if they didn't care, and life was still rolling by."

I have never forgotten those words, because it's true: Life does keep going, no matter who dies, no matter what happens. It keeps going with or without us. The dynamics of our lives changed that day. We were in another dimension; another world that we would have to learn to live in; and we would all have to adapt and become part of it.

The original name of this chapter was "Treacherous Waters," but a couple of months after I wrote it, I was sifting through my Bible for a specific verse for another chapter, and my eyes glazed across Simon of Cyrene on the page. It was the day of Christ's crucifixion. I knew exactly where it needed to be. It had to be the title of this chapter. It was fitting.

Mark 15:21 says: *"They compelled a passer-by, who was coming in from the country, to carry his cross; it was Simon of Cyrene, the father of Alexander and Rufus."*

I can imagine Simon and his two sons coming back into town from the country, tired from their journey and seeing droves of people in the streets from a distance. They look up at the sky above the town, dark clouds looming, ready to lay burden on the people.

As they sift their way through the crowd toward the commotion, they hear some cheering, and some wailing in sorrow, like two competing sides. They reach the center street in town only to see a spectacle, a horrible example of human nature at its worst: Jesus collapsing under the weight of the cross, being led to his death. Simon and his sons feel the weight of the burden he is carrying and are sorrow-stricken. Simon feels a tight grip on his arm and a hard yank pulling him into the street toward Jesus and the cross. Bewildered, he naturally pulls back, but can't get away; now there are two Roman soldiers dragging him. They take the cross from Jesus and heap the weight of it onto Simon's shoulders and force him to carry it and follow Jesus to Calvary.

Why him?

There are three accounts of this in the Bible: In Matthew it says he was compelled to carry the cross, in Mark it refers to Simon as a passer-by, and in Luke it says he was seized and made to carry the cross. But one thing they have in common in all three accounts: There was no reason for them to pick him. He wasn't guilty of anything. They had no reason to single him out and yank him from the crowd and make him part of the unthinkable. But that didn't matter. It was his turn to be picked.

The day of the accident we learned that life is cruel sometimes, and that we can be innocent as doves and be picked, yanked, seized, and compelled to carry the cross. It doesn't matter if we are a ten, thirteen, or sixteen-year-old child; it doesn't matter if we are a son, a daughter, a father, or a husband minding our own business in life. That burdensome cross can be heaped onto our shoulders, and its weight and jagged edges can come crashing down cutting all the way down to the quick of our heart, through no fault of our own.

We learned that day that there are times in life when we are that innocent passer-by, called to be Simon.

16

The Funeral

A week went by like a thick fog obscuring the light. Eva was recovering and was moved from Bakersfield to a rehab facility in Visalia. My nephews and brother-in-law were out of the hospital. Dad and I made the arrangements for the funeral. We decided to have them both together on the same day. Sitting in the funeral home with the director was not a place I ever imagined I would be. He sat across from us asking us a litany of questions, trying to help us give Mom and Mary the best sendoff. But one question he asked, I'll never forget: "Do you want open caskets?"

We knew Mom's would be okay. But Mary was in the passenger's seat, and she died of blunt force head trauma. "Do you think it would be wise to have her casket open?" I asked him. I couldn't ask him how she looked. I just couldn't say those words.

He knew exactly what I meant. "I can do my best to help her, but..." He paused, raising his palms.

I reached over and put my hand on Dad's forearm. "We can't let the kids see their momma that way." Dad just shut his eyes and rocked his head up and down.

He asked us if we wanted to see her, and we both shook our heads no. The last image I had of her, she was smiling and waving to me, saying, "Love you too." I didn't want to change that.

He gave us the dates available and the only one that would work was August 30. "We can't do it on the 30th, Dad," I told him. "That's Eva's birthday."

He rubbed his pant legs and turned toward me. "We have no choice, we'd have to wait another week if we don't. I don't want to have it on that day either, but we have to," he said.

August 30 was Eva's sixteenth birthday, a milestone in a young girl's life that was thwarted by the unthinkable. But that day wasn't just a milestone for Eva, it was one for Mom and Dad too. It would have been their fortieth anniversary, a milestone in itself. It was the day he married the girl that was born in Oakland, California, that somehow made it to Delano and was sitting on the porch the day Dad walked by and their eyes first met. It was the worst day for a funeral. But you do what you must sometimes.

We set the date and made the arrangements with the church. We had a lot of help from the family and the community. We knew there was going to be a massive amount of people because they were well-known and, more than that, they were loved by everyone. Thursday came, August 29, the night of the Rosary. The night was a blur, but crystal clear. It was the beginning of goodbye.

The church was overflowing. People stood piled

in all the doorways and lined two to three deep in the aisles and flowed out of the church. It was hot inside the church, but the burning loss inside us was worse. Every single person in the church died a little that night, a part of them was lost.

My brother-in-law and my nephews sat in the front row. I'll never forget the look on their faces. Lost, bewildered, doesn't even come close. But there was one more person suffering that couldn't be there: Eva. She was still in the rehab facility and not able to come

The two caskets that sat in front of the altar lay silent beside each other. The architect that designed the church had one casket in mind. I don't think he or she ever imagined two. It was evident. Even the building moaned, saying, *This is not supposed to happen, there is never a time when two caskets should lay side by side. It's not right.*

Mary and Mom lay silent inside their temporary home, but the hundreds of people surrounding them sung beautiful songs to them, joined by the angels helping them on their way. People stood in front testifying to their goodness and the love they spread. It was a beauty that overshadowed the reality of the tragedy for a few hours.

The funeral the next day spoke volumes of them. There were so many people and cars the local police department came to escort everyone to the cemetery. The sendoff they received was inspiring. It's still a comfort to think back to being at the cemetery and looking around at the sea of people that came to let everybody know that they loved Mom and Mary too. A profound testament to two lives lived well. But there was someone missing. Eva. It was her sixteenth birthday, a special time in a young girl's life, turned into something it should have never been. There would be no family surrounding her with smiles and pride; there would be no candles lit with family singing Happy Birthday to a beautiful daughter, granddaughter, niece, and friend. She wouldn't get that hug from two proud parents and brothers that loved her; she would have to lie alone, broken, living an unfathomable loss.

Dad and I stayed after the burial rites, we wanted to watch them lower the caskets and say our goodbyes. Everyone else went to the city park to the reception. We had to have it there because there wasn't any other place big enough in Lindsay that could hold so many people. As soon as everyone left the workers from the cemetery came to do their part. We watched them lower two people loved by many. I can still hear the ratchet sound as both caskets descended to their place of rest. To a place where there are no more goodbyes.

17

Not Equipped

Not knowing what to do is an awful thing, especially when it's something so serious. Eva was released from rehab, and she and my brother-in-law and two nephews came to stay with us so Cristy could help Eva. Cristy is an LVN. I realized something real fast. We needed something bad: Mom and Mary. We were all at a loss and trying to find our way. Everyone in our house had suffered. I know we aren't the first family to suffer tragedy, but it was a first for us, and it did feel like the world around us was collapsing.

The kids needed their Grandma Sara. They needed to see that soft, beautiful smile that taught so many to love. My kids needed their Tia Mary. They needed to hear her laugh, they needed to see the energy she had bursting at the seams and zest for life that she shared with them so many times. Eva, Beni, and Vicente needed their momma. They needed her to be there. They needed her to hug them and tell them that life was still normal and that they would be okay. They needed to hear her say they could be anything they wanted to be and to not give up, that she is always with them. Louie needed his wife to help him raise and guide their children. He needed her energy and drive to cope with what lay ahead. He needed her to tell him how to be both mother and father to their children. Cristy needed them both too. As much as she wanted to, she could never replace what Mom and Mary were to them. All she could do was her best. I love her for that.

We did our best to keep living and functioning. There are things about their stay with us that stand out. My middle nephew, Beni, and I stood outside our house one day and he told me he had a dream about his mom. He told me his mom was on an inner tube in the water and was trying to get to the shoreline where he was, but the current was too strong. No matter how hard she tried to get to him, it kept taking her farther away. What an awful dream for a young boy. He had already lost her in real life, only to lose her in his dreams too. I don't remember what I said to him when he told me, but I do know I didn't know what to say. Even today, it would be hard to find the words he needed to hear, but this I could tell him with confidence: his mom is still with him in his heart, and she's still guiding him. I can say this because she is still in mine, never to be lost.

A couple of years before the accident I started reading the Bible and studying daily. I had a routine. I would get up at 4:30 a.m. and study. I still have a routine, but now I get up at 4 a.m. and split my time between studying and writing. While they were staying with us, I kept my schedule. When I studied, the only light on in the house was the desk lamp that illuminated the Bible in front of me. Almost every morning my youngest nephew, Vicente, would come out of the darkness and put his arm around me. "I miss my mom, Nino," he would tell me. "All I want is one more hug. I want to tell her I love her, that's all I want."

It broke my heart then, and it still does. What do you say? How do you respond? All I could say was, "I miss her too, *Mijo* (son). I wish I could hug her too." But he never did get that hug from her, only those in his memories.

There was someone else that was lost in everyone else's misery, invisible in a sense. Dad. I don't think any of us gave his feelings a lot of thought. But, as it happens, sometimes we see more clearly looking back. Maybe it's what we do in times of crisis to protect ourselves from being overwhelmed. Today I see him clearly. I see him here at our house with all of us, trying to find normalcy, then going home in the evening, alone, with no one to comfort him. He lost his daughter, his Maria, his firstborn; he lost his partner; and he buried them both on his fortieth wedding anniversary. He went home to an empty house and suffered alone every night. I never thought about how lonely he was, and all the times he cried into the dead air surrounding him, wondering if he could ever wake up from the horrible dream he was living through.

I could have been better. I could have opened my eyes wider and tried to understand what the kids and Dad were going through. But I guess I could only give the best I had at the time. I know now what I really needed: I needed the two girls we all lost. They always knew what to do and what to say in any situation. They knew how to make everything better. We all needed them, but they were gone, and we would have to learn how to move forward and catch up with the world still in motion around us. Without them.

18

The Rose

The years passed, and my brother-in-law Louie learned how to be both mom and dad in his household. He did what he needed to do to survive — and so did the kids. Cristy and I did the same. Dad was busy all the time; he took the kids to all their doctor's appointments and wherever they needed to be when my brother-in-law couldn't take them. He was trying to fill the shoes of their momma and grandma. He would do anything to fill his day. He was always over at my house trimming trees, bushes, pulling weeds. They were things that seemed insignificant to me. "Dad, you don't have to do those things, they don't matter," I'd tell him. I didn't understand what he was trying to do. I couldn't see the obvious.

I still went to his house every day for lunch, like I did when Mom was alive. It was the same thing every day. He would tell me every single thing he did that day. I mean everything. He would tell me he was thinking about going to the casino, that he had a new strategy. He would tell me about every single bush and blade of grass he cut. Trivial. All trivial to me. But one day it was different, not so trivial. I walked in the front door and he wasn't sitting at the dining room table like he usually was, waiting for me. He was sitting in the TV room on the sofa. This is how our conversation went:

"Hey, Pop, how's it going?" I said, ready to hear every single detail of his day — the trivial — and the even more trivial.

"Hey, son, I've been waiting for you. I have something important to tell you."

I was standing in the doorway leaning against the doorjamb looking down toward him, "Yeah, Dad, what's up?"

He crimped his lips and raised his eyebrows, "I met someone, and I really like her."

"What are you talking about?" I raised my voice. The feeling of anger billowed up ready to take control of my vocal cords. "What the hell? Mom wasn't good enough for you? Her memory is not enough? All you do is the same damn thing every day. I don't care about the bushes you trim or your new strategy for the casino. Why don't you talk about something that means something? That's why you're out looking for something you don't need."

I was pointing and flinging my hand at him the whole time. He sat there with his head down, not saying a word, just nodding his head slowly, letting me rant. "What's wrong with you?" I said, as I turned to leave. I left him sitting stooped over on the sofa, alone, as he had been since Mom died.

I went home and told Cristy about it. She just listened, without a word.

A few days went by and I still went to see him at lunchtime. Neither of us talked about what had happened a few days before. I couldn't see the elephant in the room if it was sitting on me. On Friday of that same week, I was home working around the house in the front yard. My daughter Sara was with me playing in the yard. She told me after reading this chapter that she remembered the day clearly. Tia Josie pulled up in her red Camry. She had become like a stand-in for Mom, my go-to for guidance. She and Mom did everything together. They were the example of what all brothers and sisters should be, always there for each other, and close. They weren't twins, but they were inseparable. They even bought the same kind of cars.

"Hi, Tia," I said as she came toward me.

"Hi, *Mijo*," she said, giving me a hug. She took a step back and put her hands on my shoulders and looked right into my eyes. "Robert," she said, "you really hurt your dad the other day."

"Why?" I said, stepping back until her hands slid off my shoulders.

"When you chewed him out, you hurt him."

"Well, why does he need to date or marry anyway? Mom wasn't good enough?"

"You know she was. You know that she was more than a lifetime of love for him. But it is possible to fall in love again. Look at your mom. She loved so many people and always had room for more in her life. She knew that love crosses all boundaries, and I know that she wouldn't have wanted your dad to be alone. His wanting to fall in love again is a testament to the life he had with her."

My heart started to sink. The elephant in the room I was ignoring was sitting on me now. I couldn't ignore it anymore. The reality that Dad went home to an empty house every day, all alone, hit me. All the trivial things I criticized him for were all he had to fill the gaping hole in his life. Dad suffered the absolute worst fate of all, he lost a child and the love of his life all in one day. "I know, Tia. You're right. I know Mom would want him to be happy." I felt horrible about everything I'd said to him. I kicked my own dad while he was down. "I'm gonna go talk to him right now," I told her.

"Good," she said, hugging me.

I hopped into my truck after she left and headed to Dad's. It's only five minutes from my house to his, but it was long enough for my heart to sink to its lowest level. Every horrible thing I said a few days before became crystal clear. I'd never talked to Dad that way in my whole life. I never had a reason to and I didn't in this situation either. On the way over, something happened. The loss of Mom and Mary crashed down on me, and I got a glimpse of the pain he suffered with their loss.

I was glad it was only a five-minute drive. I felt like my heart was being dragged on the pavement under my truck on the way. I found him sitting on the same spot where he'd been the day of my rant. I didn't even say hi to him, I went straight to the apology for all the rotten things I said. I told him I was glad he found someone he cared about.

He smiled and stood up and hugged me. "Don't worry about it, son," he said.

He forgave me in a second, for one of the worst things,

in my eyes, I had ever done. "What's her name, Dad?"

"Her name is Rose," he said, happy he could tell me about her.

They went on to marry in January of 2002, and we had a new beginning in our family. A different chapter. Rose had a son and a daughter who became my new brother and sister. We had one thing in common: I had lost my mom in a car crash, and they lost their father in a motorcycle accident. The only difference was I had more time with Mom. Their dad died when they were one and three years old.

This wasn't another curve ball life threw our way, it was just a new twist in our life. It was something new that I, and I'm sure they as well, had to get used to. But it didn't take long. Dad and Rose chose well, which made it easy. She moved into my childhood home where I grew up, but within a year they bought another home just across town. A fresh start. We still have the old house, never to be sold because too many good memories live there.

When Rose came into Dad's life, it ultimately gave

me relief. It gave me a new sense of freedom. I didn't have to walk around with guilt scratching at the back of my neck all the time. "Is Dad okay? Should I invite him over for dinner? Is he lonely?" I had those thoughts and many more, constantly. If Dad had been a horrible father, maybe it would have been easier, and I wouldn't have had any guilt. But he was the best. I couldn't have been more blessed, so feeling guilty was the least I could do. But he married and was happy — and so was I.

Cristy and I had a new beginning too. We got back to camping. We love the coast. We were free to do whatever we wanted without the feeling of leaving someone behind. Cristy loved Dad, so she wore a lot of the same guilt I did. I guess guilt is proof of love sometimes. But both Dad and I were enjoying a new beginning. No one had to feel guilty anymore.

19

T.I.A.

It was a regular Sunday. Dad got up early to have his coffee — nothing out of the ordinary. He started his usual routine, getting geared up for church. His first step was his shave and trimming his trademark mustache; thick and hanging just over his lip. I wish I could grow one like him.

He got ready, and he and Rose headed to church for the 9 a.m. mass. They sat in the same spot they always did, like most people do. Church was always the first order of the day on Sundays. They never missed. But this wouldn't be a normal Sunday. He was sitting listening to the homily of the day and slouched both forward and sideways at the same time, like someone pulled the batteries out of him. His body was limp. Everyone's first assumption was heart attack. Someone called the ambulance, but by the time they came he was better, like someone put the batteries back in. We took him to a heart specialist, who said Dad was having TIAs (Transient Ischemic Attack, also known as a transient stroke or mini stroke). A TIA usually only results in short-term symptoms. The doctor found that Dad had a leaky valve in his heart. He recommended surgery, but Dad didn't want anything to do with it. His first response to it was "No." But he had a few more TIAS, seemingly all at church, and finally relented. He agreed to have the leaky valve fixed.

We set the date, and he had the surgery at UCLA Medical Center. It was successful; they fixed the valve and a small hole in his heart. They let us stay in the ICU with him. He was in excruciating pain that they couldn't relieve. All night he moaned, "Help me, Lord." It was hard for me to watch. In all my life I had never seen Dad at the mercy of any situation. He was always in control and had never stepped foot in a hospital unless it was to visit someone. But that night, he suffered like nothing I'd ever seen.

He recovered from the surgery, and we brought him home. It was a slow recovery, but he was getting better. In our minds we had fixed the problem. *No more TIAs, he'll get better and we'll get back to normal*, we thought. Now, years later, I think about the day of the surgery and the way he agonized. I can't help but think that it took something from him that day. It took that spark he had, that brightness in his eyes had dimmed a little — and I knew it. I just didn't know what it meant for the future.

Today, I wonder how much we should try to intervene with letting nature take its course. I remember the first time I had those thoughts. I imagined slapping myself because it sounded terrible to me. How could I not try to extend my father's life? What a terrible son. But I realize today that we made the best decision we could at the time with the information we had. If we could have seen the future, I'm sure Dad would have made a different choice. His heart was strong now, but what about the rest of him?

20

The Stroke

It was December 2, 2013. A normal day, I thought. My cell phone rang. It was Dad's home number on the screen. "Hello," I answered.

"There's something wrong with your dad." It was Rose.

I was there within five minutes. I live less than a mile from his house. I rushed inside and found him lying on the bed with his eyes open. The best I can describe the expression on his face is disoriented. I asked him how he was feeling and got no response. We called 911, and the ambulance was there within minutes. They loaded him up and rushed him to the closest hospital, about twenty-five minutes away, in Visalia, with a possible stroke. We followed. The lights flashed, signaling that someone was sick inside and needed to get to the hospital fast.

A couple of weeks before, Cristy and I ran into him at the local grocery store, nothing out of the ordinary. After we left, she told me, "Something's not right with your dad. He doesn't look right."

I didn't see it. I brushed it off and moved on with my day, but there was something brewing. I never imagined that in a couple of weeks I would be following an ambulance with him inside.

They rolled him into the emergency room with us following in lockstep. They connected wires to him with stickers to hold them in place to monitor his vitals. Shortly after that they whisked him away to get a CT scan of his brain. Thirty minutes later a doctor walked in. "Our suspicions were correct. He had a stroke and a massive brain hemorrhage in the back of his head."

"What can we do?" we asked.

"We are sending him to another hospital in Fresno, they're better equipped to handle something like this."

We agreed and followed the ambulance to Fresno, about forty-five minutes away. The ambulance turned into the parking lot of Community Regional Medical Center, and we entered our second hospital of the night. It was busy and packed with lots of people in the waiting room, lots of staff, and lots of security. Everyone coming into the hospital had to go through an intense security checkpoint before coming in. I looked around at some of the people already inside and thought, *Maybe they should run some of these people through the security check one more time, just to be safe.*

We couldn't see Dad. They had rolled him into an elevator and disappeared. We had to wait in one of the waiting rooms in the lobby. That in itself was an interesting place to be. The people in there went from clean-cut to rough-cut, and possibly gangster. Sorry.

Family slowly started showing up to see how Dad was doing, and to give us their support. About thirty minutes later they came and got us. We went up to the third or fourth floor and the doors opened. *Oh my God*! I thought. It was like someone turned the volume up, times ten. It was loud. Nurses and doctors buzzed up and down the halls, and patients on gurneys were strewn all over the place. They lined the walls with no gaps. Makeshift rooms with curtains for walls filled the whole area. It looked like a MASH unit in the military. They ushered us to one of the makeshift rooms and pulled the curtain back. Dad lay there weak, not even able to wonder what was going on. He always knew what to do in any situation, and what his next move would be. But not that night. It was different. The signals and usual way his brain fired wasn't working.

Rose and I stood looking at him with multiple conversations going on outside the curtain discussing a multitude of other patients' problems. Dad's problems were overshadowed by the many others in the hospital. He wasn't the only one that needed attention, but as his son, I felt that all hands and eyes should be on Dad, trying to help him. But it doesn't work that way, I learned.

Wires wove their way in and out of Dad's hospital gown and to their respective machines. Beeps and alarms were constantly sounding off joining the choir of all the other machines that surrounded us. His eyes were open, but as the old cliché goes, nobody was home. They would come in every fifteen minutes to ask him questions.

"What's your name?" they'd ask.
"I don't know."
"Where do you live?"
"I don't know."

"What year is this?"

"1920."

The nurse pointed to me. "Who's this?"

He looked at me, seemingly scanning his brain searching for a good connection. Something to confirm and reveal who this man was. "I don't know," were the words that finally rolled out of his mouth softly, almost apologetic, because he knew it was an important question.

It felt weird to hear him say that. He named me when I was born, how could he forget? But I knew enough about strokes to know that it happens. I just didn't know if it would be permanent.

Doctors were in and out, rushing from patient to patient, each with their own unique problem. Eventually one came in to see him and said he was going to order an MRI to get a better look at the possible damage he might have suffered. We were glad. Not knowing leaves too much room for speculation and overactive imaginations.

Rose's grandson Noah came into the ICU with us. He was an RN at Kaweah Delta Hospital in Visalia at the time, and knew people at the hospital we were in. He's a PA now, my go-to guy. They let him come up with us. The curtain slid open about thirty minutes later and they wheeled Dad out with the wires and machines trailing behind him. We waited and waited. It took forever, in patient family time.

Nobody came in to update us, so we didn't know they were having trouble getting Dad to stay still in the MRI machine. He never feared anything, but for some reason, that machine scared him that night. They gave him a shot of Benadryl and gave it time to kick in. It didn't work. They decided to give him Ativan. Big mistake. They managed to give him the MRI, but the Ativan and Benadryl triggered a reaction. Those two medications together fired up a part of his brain we would have never thought we would have seen that night in his condition. But as we know, we still have much to learn about the brain. It is, as they say: A world of its own.

When they wheeled him back into his makeshift room, he had a gleam in his eyes. A sneaky one. He grinned as his bed came to a stop.

"How you doing?" I asked.

He smiled and laughed. That's when the comedy show started. Here we were in a hospital in a serious predicament. Something in Dad's head had burst and was bleeding — a life or death situation — but you wouldn't know it. Within a minute, everyone within earshot was dying laughing. Even the nurses couldn't stop laughing. The Benadryl and Ativan triggered the funny bone in his brain. Dad always had a good sense of humor, but he wasn't comedian material. That night he could have stood in front of any crowd and had them doubled over laughing. It was almost embarrassing. Here we were surrounded by sick people and Dad was having his own little comedy show in the midst of it all.

It lasted twelve hours. He still didn't know who I was, but he came up with a new name for himself. His nickname growing up was Rocky, and when the nurses would come and ask him what his name was, he would say "Rocky the Lion," with that same grin he'd used all night.

The effects of the medication finally wore off and they moved him to a part of the hospital for people that suffered from his type of trauma. A neurosurgeon came in to see us and explained his situation. She said he had a massive brain hemorrhage and at his age it wouldn't be prudent to try any surgery. "There is a delicate line we have to walk," she said. "We have to worry about his brain continuing to bleed, and the possibility of blood clots forming. If we give him coagulants it could create blood clots, and if we don't, he could bleed out." All we could do was wait and see.

After a couple of days, he started remembering names, but he wasn't the same guy he was before the stroke. He could walk and talk. He could use the restroom on his own, and there was no physical rehab needed. Once they confirmed that the bleeding had stopped and had started drying up, they released him. They told us that the dry blood would eventually get absorbed.

It's hard to explain, but I knew life would be different for him and everyone close to him. None of us knew how, but we all knew the unknown was our future.

21

He's Home

We were happy to bring Dad home. We had survived what would be his first stroke. The neurosurgeon gave us a list of activities to do with him to try and reconnect some of the wires that were disconnected with the stroke. We didn't know yet what kind of damage he suffered. It wasn't something you could see with your eyes, it was something inside his head. It's the part of our anatomy that makes us who we are, the part that is mysteriously and undeniably connected to the human heart that makes each one of us unique. The human brain, an unfathomable mystery.

He could talk, walk, and function like most people. He knew when to go to the bathroom. He could take a shower without help. He still had his sense of humor. He still had all the capabilities most of us take for granted. But there was something off, something was going on inside his head. There was a child hidden for decades working his way to the surface.

I'll never forget the first time the child revealed himself to me. I stopped by on my morning break, and he was sitting at the kitchen table with one of those boards you buy for kids to learn their shapes in front of him. Different shapes were strewn around the board waiting to be put in the right hole.

"Hey...my son is here," Dad said.

I never used the front door in Dad and Rose's house; I always came in through the back porch. When I came through the door, wherever Dad was in the house, I would hear him say those words: "Hey...my son is here." Like a verse in a song you love to hear over and over.

"Hi, Dad," I said. "What's going on?"

He looked up at me with a proud look that a child would give a parent. "I'm doing my homework," he said, with one of the shapes raised in his hand. I knew at that moment that Dad wasn't completely Dad anymore.

As humans we want to be in control of our lives. We want to know exactly what's going on and be in control of it. We don't like change, because it disrupts our little ecosystem we've been working on our whole lives. But what Dad wasn't conscious of had revealed itself to me. It was clear. We are not always in control; uncertainty is always just around the corner. It's like driving around a blind curve in the mountains and finding a car coming in the opposite direction on your side of the road and it's too late to avoid the collision.

One by one the pieces of evidence of the effects of the stroke revealed themselves. The best way to describe it is, his mind wasn't working with or for him anymore. It was slowly becoming a mind of its own. He couldn't remember his age or what year it was, he couldn't write his name and started to lose the ability to name things common to all of us: a fork, a pencil, toothpaste, the difference between the TV remote and the phone. Some would say that those things are minor and don't really matter. They would be right in a sense, but each one of those little things combined are parts of what make us a whole person.

He was still Dad, and he still loved me. But it wasn't just him anymore. I walked over and sat next to him, and with the instinct of a parent I put my hand on his shoulder. "Good job, Dad," I told him, grabbing another shape. "Where does this one go?" He looked at the piece and the open spots on the board and kept trying until he found the right spot. "Good job, Dad. I'm proud of you," I told him, patting him on the shoulder like a parent would. I can still see the grin of satisfaction he gave me that day, just like the ones I gave him as a child.

22

I Want to Go Home

It was May 14, 2014, about 7 p.m. I was settled in and half-way lying down on my favorite sofa. I had grabbed the remote and pressed the red button, ready to let the TV have my attention. My phone rang.

"Hello," I said.

"There's something wrong with your dad," Rose said, a familiar line I'd heard before.

"I'll be right there."

I rushed over and found him with the same glazed look he had with his first stroke. The ambulance came and loaded him up and rushed him to Kaweah Delta Hospital in Visalia. It was a stroke but not as severe as the first one. He remembered our names and who we were. That was a relief. But he did develop a problem with his prostate. I don't think the stroke caused it, but that's when it started. He couldn't urinate, so they put a catheter in.

The hospital recommended that we ask him if he

would want to fill out an Advanced Directive (a patient's wishes in writing of what they do and don't want done to them if they are ill, incapacitated, or in an accident) while we were there.

He was able to understand the questions as they explained them to him. He was clear with his answers. He knew exactly what he wanted them to do in a life-or-death situation: nothing.

There were two things he would leave the hospital with: A catheter and a statement. No, I guess I should say, a declaration.

I remember sitting in his hospital room with him, and out of the blue he looked my way. "I want to go home," he said.

"You'll be home soon, Dad, they said it will just be a couple more days, and you'll be home."

He looked up at me. "I want to go home," he said again, pointing to the sky, making it clear exactly what he meant.

"You don't mean that Dad. We want you here with us."

With clarity in his eyes, "I'm not afraid, I want to go home," he said.

From that day forward, those five words — "I want to go home" — were standard procedure to hear when you were around him. He knew exactly what he wanted, and we knew it too.

That conversation reminds me of one I had with my father-in-law while Dad was in the hospital. He told me Dad told him years back that the last thing he wanted in life was to lose his faculties and become a burden to his family, and not be able to take care of himself. But that's where life had put him, in the very predicament he never wanted to be in.

Most of us try to plan every part of our lives, but as life goes on, we find that there are plans we don't know about, ones we cannot see. They are like the wind, un-seeable and unpredictable.

The hospital recommended he go to the nursing home for thirty days of rehab and we agreed. They released him after six days and sent him to the nursing home I described in the first chapter of this book. This is how the rest of that first evening in the nursing home went:

I followed the gurney as it maneuvered its way down the hall in between wheelchairs. It was an awkward feeling. Hard to explain. If you've never been in a nursing home or haven't worked in one you might not understand the sentiment I'm trying to convey. I drove by this facility a million times and never gave it a second thought, never a second of my time. I just blew by without a clue. But it was my turn to experience and see what was behind door number one.

We reached the end of the hallway and made a hard left down another one. It was clear sailing, no wheelchairs in our way. The gurney glided over the shiny floors quietly all the way to the last door next to an exit. The nurses' station looked miles away behind us. There were three beds in the room, two already inhabited. The room reminded me — still does — of calling to reserve a hotel room at the last minute and getting the last room available next to the laundry room, or one with zero view, or, as I've experienced firsthand, landing in the room next to the dog walk. But we were grateful they found a spot for Dad.

They moved him from the gurney onto the last empty

bed. He complied with no emotion, not in control of his own life anymore.

A representative from the facility came in with a stack of papers for us to go over and sign. I felt numb inside, confused about how all this might play out. Dad lay there quiet, like a puppy. The hardest thing for me that first night was going home. I was tired, nervous and didn't know how to leave. I felt like I was leaving one of my own kids at an orphanage. But I did leave, and there would be a tomorrow. Just different.

23

The Bag

We survived what would be Dad's first stay in a nursing home. Other than the stroke degrading his mind a little more, he seemed to be doing okay, with the exception of the bag strapped to his leg. He still couldn't urinate, so we brought him home with a catheter. I have to say, that bag on the side of his leg, and the catheter, was the most exhausting ailment he had, not just for him but for us too.

Dad couldn't understand the concept of a catheter. To him it was a foreign object that was stuck into one of his body parts with a bag connected to it that didn't belong. It was like having a fly on his nose with his hands tied behind his back. He instinctively wanted it out of, and off of, his body. So guess what? He pulled that annoying little thing out more times than I can count. And it always happened when our only option to get it back in was to take him to the emergency room. We waited in the emergency room countless times, for countless hours. A true nightmare.

The urologist tried everything. He tried medication; he tried every procedure he could do in his office. We were exhausted. Having a catheter is a twenty-four-hour job, especially when the person wearing it can't understand why it's plugged into him. I would be home finally settling in for the day and the dreaded phone would ring.

"Hello?"

"Your dad pulled his catheter out again," Rose would say.

My head would fall back in disbelief. "I'll be right there," I'd say, being the good soldier he taught me to be.

Within a few minutes we would be on our way to our two- to five-hour stint in the emergency room. We'd bring him home, contemplating and dreading our next trip back.

After six months of the catheter nightmare and trying every possible procedure we could, his doctor told us about a surgeon at USC Institute of Urology here in California. He said the surgeon, Dr. Mihir Desai, a good friend of his, pioneered the procedure called Robotic Simple Prostatectomy and Bladder Diverticulectomy. It's a procedure done with robotics, without removing the prostate. He asked if we would like to try it. "Heck yeah," we told him. We wondered why he waited so long to offer that option to us. We were willing to try anything.

We drove him to USC for some preliminary testing and everything was a go. On December 9, 2014, he had the surgery. It was a success. The doctor explained the procedure to us in layman's terms, saying that inside his prostate there was an overgrown forest blocking the urine from flowing freely. "We chopped that forest down," he said. "There's no more blockage."

We were relieved.

We brought him home after three days, with a catheter and a bag still strapped to his leg for the recovery time. All we had to do was keep him from pulling it out before we went back in two weeks. We made it! The catheter stayed in and we took him back and everything looked good. They pulled it out and he had no problem urinating, and our prostate ordeal was over. Thank God. We were so grateful. You wouldn't think something like that could create so much havoc in people's lives.

I remember the ride home after being cleared by the surgeon. We were all happy Dad's prostate problems were over. We put Dad in their Nissan Frontier truck and told him we were taking him home, and that he didn't have to wear the catheter anymore. He was so happy. He kept telling us, "I'm so happy to go home, I can't wait to get there."

I don't think it even registered with him that he didn't have to wear the catheter anymore, but his instinct to go home was strong.

We made it over one more bump in the road. We were bringing him home with one less problem, both for him, and for Rose and me. And all we knew was we wouldn't have to make any more late-night trips to the emergency room to put his catheter back in.

We could move on with our lives, knowing deep down that there would be more bumps in the road in our future. But hoping for the best.

24

Appreciation

It was a hot summer's day. Dad was all healed up from his prostate surgery. His walk had slowed quite a bit since his last stroke. And his foot seemed to be slowly twisting back to what it was as a child, hindering his walking ability even more. But his instinct to work was still strong, and we had a hard time keeping him from going outside to work in the yard. For some people working is a big part of their identity, part of their self-worth. That's how they know they are still in control of their own life. It's not just busy work, it's their contribution to their household.

Cristy went to the grocery store and decided to go by Dad's place one day. Rose was out getting a few things herself. She told Dad, like she always did, "Stay inside, I'll be right back."

Dad would agree, like he usually did, but would still go outside after she left.

When Cristy came around the corner, guess who was

out front? Dad had a bandana on his head, with sweat running down his cheeks, pruning one of the trees in the front yard. Cristy pulled over and he looked at her and smiled. "You're not supposed to be out here," she told him.

"I know, I know. I'll go in," he said, with the pruning shears dangling in his hand.

Cristy came home and told me what he was doing. I went over and he was still out there pruning and sweating away. When I pulled up, he had a big smile highlighting the gap between his two front teeth. "What are you doing, Dad?"

"I knew she was going to tell you," he said.

How can you get mad at that? He was doing what he loved to do. Work. Keeping his yard all tidied up was top priority. I think he could sense that some of the basic joys and staples in his life were slowly slipping through his fingers. Things we all take for granted, things that could be considered mundane or trivial, were all the things he was trying to hold onto. His instinct was to be productive and contribute to his household.

I laughed. "Yeah, she said you looked like you saw a ghost. How 'bout I get you a chair and you give me those pruning shears and you can tell me what you want trimmed."

He agreed, but that wouldn't be the last time he would be caught outside doing things he shouldn't. Eventually, I took all his ladders so I wouldn't find him on the roof. His walk was slow and fragile, but he managed to sneak out of the house quite a bit. Rose would call me. "Your dad is outside in the backyard and he won't come in. He's pulling weeds. I told him I was calling you, but he's still out there."

I'd find him on a search and destroy mission pulling dandelions. "Dad, what are you doing out here? It's too hot for you."

"Yeah, I know, but I hate these weeds," he'd say from a stooped position, ready to topple over.

I think back to that stage in his decline and how much it progressed from there. It makes me appreciate all the little things I can still do that might not mean anything to someone else but are important to me.

Each capability that Dad lost didn't just affect him, it affected Rose and me too. For each one he lost, we added one more responsibility to our to-do list. Things we never took time to appreciate, because he silently did them. But as his brain slowly lost the capacity to work with numbers and understand what was coming in the mail, and his physical abilities dwindled, everything he did quietly became loud and clear to us. It was like he had a breaker box in his head, and someone was inside turning off one switch at a time, taking one precious capability at a time away from him and handing it to us.

Not to be preachy, but if we rolled out of bed today, and we can still read the words on this page, or prune a bush, or understand the bills that come in the mail, we're doing pretty good. Think about what's next on your list to do today after you close this book and imagine if you couldn't do it anymore. Think about how important that one little insignificant thing is and be grateful for the day because you can still do it.

25

Mr. Toad's Wild Ride

Dad and I were driving down the road one day and I saw a car for sale down a dirt drive in an orange grove.

"Dad, there's a car for sale back there."

"Where?" he said.

"Right back there, down that dirt drive," I said, pointing back.

Dad had been looking for a car for Mary, who was sixteen already and didn't have a car or her license yet. I had been driving since I was a toddler. Not literally, of course, but in a sense. From the time I could walk, whenever Dad went to the store or anywhere else, I was glued to his side and wanted to go. I still remember standing next to him on the seat watching him drive. Back then nobody wore seat belts, they were just some annoying thing that always got in the way, so we just shoved them under the seat. It was back in a time when we didn't hear about kids getting hurt because they weren't wearing a seat belt — no Internet or cable TV, I guess.

I was a typical little boy that wanted to do whatever his dad was doing. I remember him putting my left hand on the steering wheel while he drove straight ahead one day, and that was it. Whenever we got near our car, I wanted to steer. As time went on and I got better at steering, he would let go of the wheel and I would keep the car going straight. A few years later he got a Chevy pickup. It was a four speed, and that was even better. I got to shift the gears wherever we went.

I would get up extra early every morning when he worked for the City of San Jose just so I could warm up the truck for him. Still in my pajamas, I would put my shoes on and walk by him sitting at the kitchen table eating breakfast and he would toss me the keys. It was the highlight of my day.

I was thirteen when we moved to Lindsay, and as soon as we settled in, he started taking me out to let me drive his pickup. I remember the first day we went out. He took me to the outskirts of town and pulled over by the local cemetery and started giving me instructions on how to drive. I sat there nodding in agreement with everything he was saying, but I wasn't really listening. All I could think was, *Okay, let me drive.*

We switched sides. "Okay, take your time," he said.

I put the clutch in, turned the key, put it in gear, let the clutch out slow, and pulled out onto the road. "Where do you want me to go, Dad?" I said as I was shifting through the gears.

He laughed. "Shoot, you drive better than me," he said.

All those years watching him paid off. I knew exactly

what to do when I needed to.

So now back to the Mary part of the story. Dad flipped the car around and pulled into the driveway. The car was parked in front of a rickety old house. A guy walked out as soon as we pulled in. We got out of the truck.

"*Buenos dias,*" the man said.

"*Buenos dias,*" Dad sent greetings back.

I was already looking at the car. It was a 64 Malibu SS with four on the floor. It was fire-engine red, with white vinyl seats. It was in mint condition. "*¿Cuánto quieres por el coche?* (How much do you want for the car?)" I heard Dad ask.

"*Trescientos cincuenta dólares* (three hundred and fifty dollars)," the man replied.

Dad couldn't believe the price. We took it out for a test drive and both fell in love with it. I pictured myself cruising down the road in it, but the reality was: it wasn't for me.

We got the money and bought the car. I watched Dad shift as we headed home, anticipating the first time I would get to drive it. Mary walked out when Dad and I pulled up. "How do you like your new car, *Mija*?" Dad said, out the window.

"That's mine?" she said, pointing at it.

"Yeah, c'mon, I want to take you out to drive it.

I jumped in between the bucket seats into the back, ready for the ride. Mary got in the passenger seat and looked at the gear shift with the big chrome ball on top. "I don't know how to drive a stick shift. I don't even know how to drive," she said.

"That's okay, you can learn," he said as we drove out

to the same place he took me the first time he let me drive, by the cemetery.

She traded seats with Dad, and he gave her a lengthy speech on how to drive a stick shift. "Do you get it?" he said.

"I think," she said.

"Okay, go ahead and start it."

She turned the key and the car jumped forward, throwing all of us back. I was already laughing.

"You gotta put the clutch in before you turn the key," Dad said, already looking nervous.

It was all downhill from there. I was doubled over laughing watching Dad's head fly back and forth as she went from popping the clutch to slamming on the brakes. Dad looked like a Mexican Pez dispenser with a mustache, except no candy came out. The car jerked from side to side as Mary tried to keep it on the road, shift, and work the clutch and the gas pedal all at the same time. I was sliding all over the back seat, dying laughing. I don't think I ever saw Dad so flustered in my whole life. Mary was nervous as heck, and I was having the time of my life.

Dad finally directed her toward our house. He couldn't take it anymore. She pulled up to the house and ran the front tire up onto the rounded curb and onto the grass, skidding to a stop. I was still laughing. I wasn't at Disneyland, but I was definitely on Mr. Toad's Wild Ride.

Dad reached over and turned the car off. They both sat quietly. I couldn't wipe the grin off my face, waiting to see what would happen next. Mary sat there squeezing the big red steering wheel and staring into oblivion. Dad was as white as a dark man could get. It's still a priceless picture.

Dad reached back with the keys in his hand. "Here, you teach her how to drive stick shift," he said and got out and walked into the house.

It took a while, but she finally got it. I was a little more patient.

I would inherit the Malibu in my sophomore year when they bought her a small Mustang II to go to college. I loved my Malibu and wish I still had it.

My first intention in writing this chapter was to share a funny story that involved Dad and Mary, but as I worked my way through it, I realized it had a little bit more to offer than just the funny part.

I was over at Dad's doing his yard a while back and Rose came out to talk to me. Something in our conversation triggered the memory. I started telling her about it, and she already knew the story. Dad had told her about me standing next to him going to the store and said that it was a fond memory. He remembered it exactly as I did.

I realized something: Our lives are built and made of stacks of memories. What we are and what we might become depend on them, even the ones that are idling in our subconscious.

I was just a little boy when I stood next to Dad and steered the car, but I've carried that image with me my whole life, as he did. It is one of the many he stacked in my memory banks. And one of the many ways he showed me what a father and son relationship should look like.

26

Speak While You Can

Piecing this book together in a way that you or anyone can make sense of, is difficult. How do you string a life together with all its ups and downs, its two steps forward and one step back? What about the deep dives some people endure and feel they can never find their way out of? How do you put it all together and make it mean something to someone other than the person that's living it?

My goal in this book is to share Dad's life with you in a way that makes sense. As we all know, our past has dictated our present, and our past together with our present helps us navigate our future. Throughout this book I have tried to convey his life in words strung together that express a theme, a person, and a life. I've written about his connection to Mom, Mary, Rose, his grandkids, me, his friends and family, and life in general. And I've been able to express all this in my own words, another important ability to be cherished.

After Dad's stroke and prostate surgery, not from one day to the next, but slowly, his ability to string thoughts together got harder and harder for him. His ability to speak was not affected by the stroke; his English and Spanish were perfect. But the connection between his mind and his vocal cords slowly frayed and made it difficult to convey the messages he wanted us to receive.

Every day, without exception, I would go to Dad's house to check in on him and Rose, at least two to three times a day. If I went on my 9 a.m. break, I would find him sitting at the kitchen table waiting for breakfast. He had to have his eggs every day. If I went at lunchtime, I would find him at the kitchen table waiting for lunch. And if I went at dinner time, guess where I would find him? He was a big eater. The reason I bring up his spot at the dinner table is because that's where we noticed the slow change in him. As time grew between his stroke, his ability to put thoughts together got farther and farther apart too. The connection was getting worse, slowly, but noticeable. He would be in midsentence and stop abruptly, then start up again, then stop. He would shake his head, frustrated. We would ask him, "What's wrong?"

"I don't know. It's just there," he would say, rubbing his forehead or the back of his neck — a sign of something we would learn later.

There were days he spoke perfectly, stringing thoughts together without any problem, and a few hours later, he couldn't. It frustrated him, because he knew exactly what he wanted to say but couldn't get it out. It was like he was in front of the TV with the remote in his hand flicking through the channels trying to find the right station but couldn't. "Something's not working," he'd say.

It was frustrating for us too. We wanted to hear what he had to say, because we knew it was important to him. But we were at the mercy of his limitations just like he was.

I want to turn this negative in Dad's life into something positive. It's something he taught me without words.

All his life he was able to say whatever, whenever he wanted. He could express any sentiment in a logical way. But that gift was being absorbed by the effects of the stroke. He knew it, and so did we. One more basic human capability was disappearing as he spoke.

If I had his problem right now, I wouldn't be able to write a clear enough sentence for anyone to understand. Luckily, I still can. I can express the silver lining of Dad's inability to share his thoughts in words. I can tell you that I still remember him telling me, "I love you, son," every day of my life. I can tell you I heard him tell Mom, Mary, and Rose those very same words, many times. And the most important part was that his actions always matched his words. Even if he was the most poetic, persuasive communicator, it wouldn't have mattered if his words didn't match his life. But his did. Even if I can't hear the words "I love you, son" anymore, I still hear them like an echo in my heart. He said them when he needed to say them. What stronger message can you leave in the hearts of all those who knew you when you were vibrant and able to speak? There isn't one. You've already said in action and words what matters most in life: "I love you."

27

Guardians of their Dignity

Most of us guys get up in the morning, take our shower, and line ourselves up with the mirror in the bathroom to brush our teeth and shave. We turn the water on and get it to the temperature we like and slap some of that warm water on our face. We reach down and grab the shaving cream and squirt some on our fingers and lather up all the parts of our face we want to shave. We reach down instinctively and grab our razor and without hesitation we start shaving, not giving it a second thought. It's part of our day. It's simple. But not for everybody. It was one of the first physical abilities Dad lost. He could turn the water on, he could lather his face to be shaven, he could grab the razor in his hand, but he didn't know what to do with it. He lost another ability.

Most of us don't think about not being able to shave or brush our hair. We assume that what we are doing today we'll be doing tomorrow. It's not true. It's not guaranteed the things we deem under our control today, will be tomorrow.

In time Dad lost the sense to know when to go to the bathroom. I never imagined or thought I would have to clean my dad after having an accident in his pants. I'm sure Rose felt the same way. She married a man that took care of his own business down to the most basic tasks, but life's circumstance whittled him back to a child in many ways. He was becoming more and more dependent on us, like we were of our parents when we were children.

Rose was going through the same thing at the same time I was. Whatever I was experiencing, she was living twenty-four hours a day because she lived there. In chapter twenty-two I talked about how Dad's catheter wreaked so much havoc in our lives. This would be the one thing that would create that same kind of havoc. We couldn't escape it. We had a six-foot-two man that had a gigantic appetite, that was constantly processing food like the rest of us. But he could no longer control the last part of the process, and his accidents always seemed to happen at the most inconvenient time: right before a doctor's visit, right before someone came to visit him, right before bedtime, and on and on. This one body function would rob us of so much time and energy.

We all know the old cliché: when it rains it pours. Well, that seemed to be living itself out. Along with his bathroom problem, his walking ability was deteriorating fast too. Taking a shower was no longer a simple task for him. I never imagined giving my dad a shower, but I had to, and so did Rose. I remember clearly the first time. I was so uncomfortable. I didn't want or need to see Dad that way. But as life commands, you do. It didn't take long to get used to it, and eventually it was just another part of my day. I found myself telling him: good job, Dad, you're doing a good job. I joked with him while giving him a shower. I would tell him he was a legend and his nickname was the fireman. He would crack up. He knew what I meant.

Cristy worked in a nursing home for twelve years. She told me one day that the most important thing you need to remember when caring for an elderly person, is their dignity. She said most of the time they know what's happening but can't control it. Those few words helped me consider Dad's dignity when he soiled himself at the most inconvenient time, the times when I felt like he should have known better, even though it was out of his control. That one word, dignity, stuck in my head. Thankfully. And when Dad was apologizing for putting me in that situation, it helped me say, "It's no problem, Dad, don't worry about it. That's what I'm here for, Pop."

I see clearly now, when someone gets to the point that they can't be the people they used to be by no choice of their own, the people that love them need to be the guardians of their dignity.

I started this chapter with Dad forgetting how to shave, because it was something that moved me. All of us know the feeling of being moved. In fact, some of us look for things, places, books, churches, or people that move us. I'm one of those people too. I love being moved. I hope one day I can be one of those people that move others toward the good in life with my writing.

Sometimes those moments come in the simplest of situations. Some might say, "What's the big deal about shaving your dad?" It really isn't that big of a deal. But there are moments in life, small ones, big ones, that change you. God touches your heart with something that really matters that all the money in the world couldn't buy.

I don't know if it was the first time or the fifteenth, but one day I came to Dad's house and found him sitting in his living room and noticed his face looked a little scrubby. "How 'bout I give you a little shave, Pop?" I told him.

"I guess," he said, one of his favorite responses.

I helped him to the bathroom and stood him in front of the sink, I put some goop on his hair and combed it first. "Okay, Pop, let's get you looking nice and handsome for Rose." He smiled into the mirror. I lathered his face up and started shaving. He always had a thick mustache that hung just over his top lip. His trademark. I was running the razor down the sides of his face and noticed him staring into the mirror in front of him. I looked toward the mirror and he was looking at me. At that moment I was catapulted back more than fifty years to when it was me standing on a stool watching him comb my hair in the mirror's reflection. I instantly remembered the smell of the Groom & Clean gel he used on my hair and the way his fingers felt gliding over my scalp. I remembered the pocket door between our two bathrooms in San Jose, and Mary standing on a stool herself watching Mom braid her hair in the mirror's reflection too.

Life had gone full circle. I was taking care of Dad like he took care of me. In that moment, on that day when I found myself remembering, I was given something that no one else could have given me. A memory. A moment in time. A snapshot of my life when it was perfect. A time when Mom and Dad were a young, healthy couple, and Mary and I were two of the happiest kids in the world. We had the best life could offer: a complete, happy family.

28

The Vitals

One of the things you learn when caring for a husband, wife, father, or mother, is you need to find humor in the situation. If you only focus on what is ailing them and consuming you, in a sense, you can go crazy.

Humor, like tears, is a release. They have different qualities, but they both work in the same way. They are like the temperature and pressure relief valve on a water heater. When life gets too tough, or too painful, and its pressures unbearable, a good laugh or a few tears shed can relieve a lot of stress.

As time went on, our time with Dad seemed to be getting gobbled up by his situation. Dad and I always joked before he started declining, but not like we did (I should say "I did") when he started getting more and more dependent on us.

Humor gave Rose and me an avenue to relieve the stress of taking care of him. None of what was happening was his fault. We knew it and would tell him so on the days he told us he was sorry we had to take care of him. We knew he was at the mercy of his inabilities.

But, as you know, if we let him, God will help us find our way. We might not have thought that humor would play such a big part in taking care of Dad, but it did. It was one of the little things that helped us cope with the fact that some days we were stuck in the mud and couldn't get out. It helped us smile when nothing was funny. It made Dad laugh on the days his mind was clear and he understood the predicament he was in. It helped him smile on the days he knew what he wanted to say but couldn't. Thankfully, he never lost that gift.

Sometimes I would joke with (pick on) Dad so much, he would tell me when he still could, "Isn't it time for you to go home?"

We made light of a bad situation. We, in a sense, fought fire with fire. Without humor, three people could have gone into a deep depression over one person's problems. But we used what God gave us. The ability to laugh.

Dad did things that dug up little treasures from the past, memories that I could laugh about with him and Rose. Out of his plight precious gems would come.

One day he had an accident right before bed. I got him cleaned up and showered and Rose got his bed and clothes ready. We got him into bed, and I sat with him. Rose and I were tired. She didn't tell me she was, but I could see it. It was another day spent doing the same thing.

She was picking up the bathroom while I talked, and I saw her going by with a towel. It dug up a memory. "Rose, have I ever told you the vitals story?"

She walked into the bedroom with the wet towel I used to dry Dad. "Vitals story?" she questioned.

"Yeah, it's the story of the time Dad taught Mary and me how to take a shower."

Dad rolled his eyes. He remembered. Rose came into the room to hear the story.

"I might have been five or six at the time. Dad called me and Mary to the bathroom. He pointed toward the shower. 'I'm going to show you kids how to take a shower,' he said.

"Mary and I thought it was funny already. We just looked and each other and smiled, waiting. He went through every detail: how to warm the water, how to use the soap, how to rinse, and, lastly, how to dry ourselves off. Mary and I were already giggling because of his demonstration on how to use the soap.

"He grabbed the towel. 'Now this is how you dry yourself,' he said, putting the towel back down. He pretended to pick up the dirty clothes on the floor and said, 'You use your dirty clothes to dry your vitals,' pretending to dry his vitals with imaginary clothes.

"That was it! 'He said vitals!' Mary said laughing. I was already doubled over laughing. 'The vitals!' we kept saying."

Rose laughed. "Now I know," she said. "I always wondered why your dad's clothes were so wet when I pulled them out of the hamper."

The three of us laughed. It relieved the pent-up pressures of the day.

A funny thing, though: if you remember in chapter three, I talked about my uncle Steve telling me about their mom making all seven of them take a bath in a tin tub with the same water, and only one towel. Before he told me that story, I told him the story I just shared with you. As I told him he laughed and rocked his head back and forth in agreement because it was exactly what they did as kids growing up. He remembered them using their clothes to dry themselves before they used the one towel. It was funny all over again. It was like a joke with a seventy-five-year-old punchline.

I think about that evening with Rose and Dad and realize that it all had meaning. It seemed like someone planned the whole thing; like it was purposely started seventy-five years ago when dad was a kid to serve a purpose on that night Rose, Dad, and I needed relief. There were too many things working together to say it was just a coincidence.

It took Dad and Uncle Steve's childhood; Mary and me learning how to take a shower; Dad's situation in his old age; and Rose wondering why Dad's clothes were wet coming out of the hamper all the time to bring it all together for a meaningful purpose. I know who planned and put it together for us that night, and I am grateful.

29

His Hands

We walk through life wishing we had said things to people before it was too late, wondering why we never told them. Why is it that we all have things we want to tell people, but don't? The words just stay on the edge of our lips piling up waiting to do what they were intended to do — change someone's life, let them know they meant something to us, settle a squabble that's gone on too long for no reason — or to just say the simple, powerful words "I love you," which have set countless lives back on course throughout history.

When Dad was still home, we had a routine. I would go over to his house around 6:30 p.m. to help get him ready for and tucked into bed. Some days I wished I could stay home and sit on my own sofa in my own house and not go anywhere, but I'm glad I didn't. Looking back on every single evening I was there; I wouldn't trade one of them for a million dollars.

Rose and I would get him all fixed up and ready for

bed. We would help him onto the bed, joking with him, as we always did, of course.

The edge of the bed beside him was my spot. I'd sit and talk with him, and he always grabbed my hand and held it. I remember the first time he did it. Cristy and I were over visiting, watching TV with him. I always sat right next to him on the sofa on the same spot. Out of the blue one day he reached over and grabbed my hand. I felt a little uncomfortable for a few seconds, until I saw Cristy look over toward me and smile. She told me later that she thought it was so cute.

I'm sure I held Dad's hand thousands of times as a child, but this was different. It was his way of telling me he appreciated and loved me.

How many eighty-year-old fathers and their fifty-five-year-old sons hold hands? We did. It's an image burned into my heart. Most men that might be reading this can't imagine sitting, standing, or in any other position holding their father's hand in an affectionate way. But I can say I had the privilege of doing it many times, so many times that I didn't wait for him to initiate, I naturally reached out to hold his hand.

Some of our best conversations were at his bedside. We didn't talk about the current news or who was running for president. He didn't care. He was at a point in his life where only things that really mattered were important. He loved hearing about his grandchildren and how well they were doing. He loved hearing about any new projects I was working on at home, because that's what he loved to do. He was always doing something around his house when he could.

But there was another subject that came up every

evening: dying. "I'm ready to go. I'm not afraid," were the words that always started the conversation. Talking about death is not a common conversation piece, but it was always on the table with Dad. If there was a T-shirt made to describe Dad's attitude toward death, it would read "NO FEAR." I know there's already shirts out there with those same words, but they best describe Dad's sentiments. Rose didn't like to hear him talk about death. She usually went to watch TV while we talked.

So there our conversation would go, to the unknown. We got to the point that we would joke a lot about it. It became everyday talk to me too. I would ask him on occasion, "If you died today what would you want to say to your family?" Some days he would give answers that were jumbled and didn't make sense, but there were days when his mind was firing on all cylinders. He would give me great things to say to his grandkids, to his family, and to me. I wish I would have recorded him every time I asked him that question. There were many days I wished the rest of his family could have been with me sitting on his bed to hear what he told me. What he said was always simple, lasting and contained his love for all of us. He always mentioned his love for God and his gratitude for his life. "I have no complaints," he'd say. "God has blessed me with a good life." He never said, *I wish I could have done this or that*, or *I wish I had more time*.

While holding Dad's hand, I learned a lot. He taught me that death should not be feared. And through his life he showed me why it should be that way. He shared the simple formula to living a complete life, no matter the years.

In the beginning of this chapter I mentioned the importance of words we keep to ourselves that should be shared with others. There were no words piled up on the edge of Dad's lips, he said what he needed to those he loved and those he met. And I was one of the lucky ones that was on the receiving end of those words. I'll never forget the wisdom that passed through his rough, warm hands into mine; those great moments shared between a father and son that some search for their whole lives; the moments that are not fleeting, that last a lifetime. An eternity.

30

Looking for a Solution

Most of us go through life living as we see fit and make decisions for tomorrow based on our own time and lives. But it doesn't always work that way. Sometimes life decides what it is you are going to do tomorrow, without your consent.

Everything seemed to be getting more complicated. Time in Rose's life was being gobbled up caring for Dad. Rose, as I've mentioned, is small compared to Dad, and day by day her ability to take care of him was getting harder and harder. Small tasks for most of us were becoming huge mountains for her to climb. Getting him into the bathroom, getting him into the shower, getting him changed and into bed was no small task. Her whole day consisted of what was the next thing Dad might need. She couldn't leave him alone; she couldn't just go to the grocery store to pick up a few things like the rest of us. She couldn't tell Dad she was going to see her new great-grandchild, she couldn't say, "I'm going to go see my daughter, I'll be back in a couple of hours." That option wasn't on the table unless I was able to come over.

Every day there was a new bar put on the windows and doors keeping her inside their house. She never complained to me about taking care of Dad, but I knew it was taking its toll on her. She wasn't far behind Dad in age and taking care of him was exhausting sometimes. I would come over and she would have a terrible cold or just be so tired she could barely keep her eyes open. Dad had a lot of problems but working a fork at the dinner table wasn't one of them. There were days that I'd find her with her head down on the table exhausted, and Dad eating away next to her not aware of how tired his wife was. But she never gave up, she always gave the best of herself to Dad, down to the last drop. A testament to her love for him.

Cristy and I love to camp, but since 2012, after Dad's first stroke, our tent trailer remained closed. It seemed that every time we had plans or booked a hotel at the coast, something would happen with Dad and our plans would have to be canceled. Eventually we gave up planning for fear of them being canceled and the disappointment we felt every time it happened. I never complained to Rose, and she never complained to me, but we are both human, and even though we both loved Dad, I know there were days that we both had the same sentiment: What about me? What about my life?

There were days when I would come home from Dad's and tell Cristy I felt like I was being robbed because I couldn't just come home. "I just want to come home," I'd tell her. "I want to be able to go on vacations and travel. It's not fair. When Mom and Dad were our age, they were traveling everywhere, enjoying life. "It's not right that all our friends are having fun traveling and doing whatever they want, and we're stuck." I'd say.

I know Cristy had the same sentiments, but she mostly kept them to herself. Still, I have many memories of her crying because our plans were canceled, or because we were invited by friends to go somewhere or do something fun and we had to tell them we couldn't go.

One day my Tia Josie stopped by to see Dad while I was there and when she was going to leave, I walked her out to her car. Before she got in, she turned and put her hands on my shoulders. "How are you doing?" she asked me.

I unloaded. "I'm at wit's end. I'm so tired. When I'm here I feel like I should be home, when I'm home I feel like I should be here. I feel like Dad is sucking the life out of me. Cristy and I should be traveling enjoying our lives, this is not what Mom and Dad did when they were our age. I'm always on a timed schedule. I can never just go home," I said all at once.

I felt horrible. I apologized for complaining about Dad. I didn't want to be that person. I wanted to be the perfect, selfless son. But she helped me realize something. She squeezed my shoulders. "You're only human, *Mijo*. It's not easy what you're doing. You're a good son."

She helped me realize that I was only human, and we can only do better and try our best to do what is good.

That day it became clear to me it was time to start thinking of other options. I knew it was time to consider putting Dad in a nursing home, not just for Rose's sake and safety, but for his too. It was no longer practical for me to try to work full-time, help take care of Dad, and try to have any form of the marriage I yearned for. Cristy loved and stood by me, always trying to give me the support I needed, but she's human too, and the situation was taking its toll on her too. She had a husband, but not really. His mind was never really home, and his time was mostly spoken for. I couldn't make her the center of my attention, because she wasn't. Dad filled that spot.

Rose, Cristy, and I were like three eggs about to crack. I knew we had to do something. I talked to Rose and told her how I felt and that we needed to do something. I told her that it wasn't just for us, but for his safety too. "We need to consider putting Dad in a home," I told her.

Her first response was that she couldn't do that to him. She is a loyal person and didn't consider putting Dad in a home something a good wife would do. But as time went on, and the more we talked about it, she agreed that it might be time. We had a problem, though. What would we tell him? How do you tell a person you love you're putting them in a home? How do you put them in the car and drive them to the nursing facility and tell them, "This is your new home"?

I came up with an idea. I would tell Dad that his doctor wanted him to go into the nursing home because he needed special care, and we couldn't give it to him (cowardly, I know). That was the plan, that was our way out, but Rose wasn't ready. The time wasn't right, so we had to wait for a sign or circumstance to help make the decision for us.

31

Last Night with Friends

It was May 16, 2017. I went to Dad's at break time, lunchtime, and after work. A normal day for the Rodriguez family. I told Rose I would be back for bedtime to help get Dad into bed. She told me the Borbons, lifelong friends of Dad's, were coming over to visit. I was happy they were coming, because Dad loved being around them. I went home contemplating going back around 7 or 7:30 to tuck him in.

I was milling around the house around 6:30 and my cell phone rang. It was Rose. "Hello?"

"There's something wrong with your dad."

"I'll be right there."

Cristy and I jumped into our truck and headed to Dad's. When we got there, he was sitting on a chair slumped over with his mouth open. "What happened?"

"We were sitting talking and laughing, having a nice visit, and from one second to the next he slumped over," Rose said.

Dad looked like someone had shut his main breaker switch off. He couldn't talk or move. The EMTs arrived right after we did. They packed him up and put him in the ambulance and we followed him to a familiar destination. The hospital.

They did a CT scan and found that he'd had a massive stroke and that he had at least four other strokes between his first stroke and his last. I remembered him rubbing the back of his head sometimes saying, "It's just there, it's just there," and not understanding what he was talking about.

He couldn't talk or respond to us talking to him. We weren't sure what would happen. The next morning a few doctors came in and gave us a couple of options. We told them that Dad didn't want any extreme measures taken to keep him alive. He was a DNR, Do Not Resuscitate. One of the doctors told us Dad's time was limited, maybe two weeks. He told us that someone would be in to talk to us about our options.

They brought some food in on a tray for us to try and feed him. He was awake, his eyes were open, but his mind was somewhere else.

Rose tried to feed him, unsuccessfully. He wouldn't open his mouth or even twitch as the fork with food pressed against his lips. Rose looked up at me. "What are we going to do if he won't eat?"

Rose measured everything by how Dad ate. She was used to putting a plate in front of him and not getting it back until it was wiped clean. I shook my head. "Nothing, Rose. Nothing." Her eyes teared up. Those weren't the words she wanted to hear, even though she knew what Dad wanted.

Rose and I were alone in the room with Dad when a lady came in. She was the hospital's case manager. She came in to give us our options. She said we could send him to a nursing home to see if they could rehab him, or we could send him home with hospice. I could still hear the doctor's words: "He has maybe two weeks."

She said they would bring a special bed and set it up in their living room.

"Rose," I said, "if Dad only has a couple of weeks, do you think he would rather pass at home? I'll stay there until he goes if we take him home." I thought I was doing what a son should do: Bring Dad home and let him pass with his family. A perfect ending to a good life. Rose agreed, and we asked the case manager to set it up for us.

After she left, everyone started coming back into the room. My in-laws, Rose's daughter and son-in-law, Tia Josie, and a few other friends and cousins. The room was full. We hadn't said anything to anyone about taking Dad home yet. The case manager came back in the room and told Rose and me that everything was arranged: transport, the bed, and everything else we would need. I could see the look on everyone's faces in the room, wondering what she was talking about.

"We're taking Dad home," I said. "The doctor said he has maybe two weeks. We think Dad would rather pass at home." Everyone looked a little shocked, like they weren't expecting to hear something like that.

Dad was lying in the center of all of us, unresponsive, and we were going to try and take him home and care for him. We got a few responses from the people in the room. "Oh, that's nice that you're going to do that."

But when I said we were taking him home I noticed

Cristy the most. Her head dropped, and I caught a glimpse of her eyes as they went down. They had the what-the-heck look on them. But she held her tongue and I was determined to take him home. It was the right thing to do, right?

Rose asked her daughter and son-in-law to go and start moving the furniture in the living room, because they were going to be putting the hospice bed in there.

Everyone left except for Rose, Cristy, and me. Rose turned toward me, "My gosh! It's your birthday, Robert." I had forgotten it was May 18. "You guys should at least go get something to eat together. I'll be alright here," she said.

We relented and headed over to the local Outback Steakhouse. I remember the drive over like it was yesterday. We were on Mooney Boulevard in Visalia and I kept seeing Cristy shaking her head in the corner of my eye. "What's wrong?" I asked her.

"Robert," she said, "it's your dad and I will back up any decision you make, but I don't think you realize what it takes to care for a person in your dad's situation." She spoke from experience.

She went down a list of things we would have to do that I hadn't really given much thought. "Yeah, but the doctor said he might last two weeks. We can handle that," I said.

She looked toward me. "That doctor isn't God, he's just guessing. I've worked with old people and seen it many times. People on their deathbed outlast the best doctors' estimates. What if that's your dad? You need a reason to send him to the hospital for three days before you can send him to a nursing home for rehab. But I'll back up any decision you make, no matter what," she said.

"That's what I want to do," I said with confidence, determined to take Dad home.

She nodded. "Okay..."

We got to the Outback and ordered our food. They brought my medium-rare ribeye steak and mashed potatoes. I'd made it about halfway through my steak when the biggest sense of nervousness I'd ever felt overwhelmed me. I was sick. Everything Cristy had said crashed down on me all at once. I reached over the table and grabbed her hand. "I screwed up. I screwed up bad," I told her.

"What?"

"I screwed up. What was I thinking? I can't take care of Dad like that at his house. I work full-time. Rose can't take care of him when I'm not there. What if he does last longer than two weeks? I'm sick. I gotta call Rose," I told her.

I called her and expressed how I was feeling and conveyed everything Cristy told me. She told me that she was feeling all the same sentiments. I asked her if it was okay to cancel bringing him home and see if he could be transferred to the local nursing home in Lindsay to be rehabbed. She agreed. I called the case manager and asked if we could change our mind and send Dad to the nursing home instead. "No problem," she said.

Maybe we weren't the first.

When I got off the phone the first words out of my mouth were, "Thank you, Jesus." I still couldn't eat my food, but I think I gave Cristy the biggest hug I'd ever given her. I was so grateful for the sound advice she gave me.

We walked down the hall toward Dad's hospital room and heard singing. It was mariachi music. We came through his door and Dad was sitting up in the bed singing in perfect Spanish. There was a tray of food in front of him and he was singing in between bites. I laughed and thanked God at the same time.

We didn't realize it yet, but God answered our prayers. We didn't have to tell Dad, "We're putting you in a home," circumstance did it for us. He needed rehab and that was the best place for him, and us. We were relieved. As much as we wanted him home, we knew it wasn't safe for Rose or for him, and that it wasn't possible for me to be there all the time. It would mark a new beginning for him in a new home and a new phase of care for him.

On the evening of May 19, Dad was wheeled into his new home. He wasn't aware of it yet and we weren't sure about it ourselves, but Rose and I had thirty days to decide. That's when Medicare would stop paying. It's a sad thing that everything boils down to money. It sways your decisions, good or bad.

He was put in a room with a gentleman named Larry who'd also had a stroke. Larry had been in a few months already, rehabbing. Dad had about twenty years on him, but they were traveling in the same boat. They were both trying to recover from a stroke. The CNA told us that he couldn't walk or talk when he first came in, that he had come a long way. She told us he would be the perfect roommate for Dad. Her prediction would become true.

Thirty days flew by and Dad had come a long way but had a long way to go. The right side of his body was still limp. We needed to decide what we were going to do now that Medicare was going to stop paying.

Our natural response was to take him home, but we knew it wouldn't be what was best for him, or us. We knew what we needed to do. It was no problem making him a permanent resident, the problem was the money. The cost for a two-person room was $6,000 a month, and more on months with thirty-one days. It's a staggering cost. Scary. How do people do it? I doubt most two-income families make that much money monthly — at least not in my part of the world. I think most of us go through life and never consider the fact that we might end up in this position. Dad's stay in the nursing home opened my eyes to many things.

We got Dad in a permanent room with Larry, who would be staying long-term too. Financially, Dad had a good retirement and social security; it would have been more than enough if he weren't in a nursing home. He had a sizeable amount of money in his checking that would help supplement what he got from his retirement. Rose and I thought it would last a couple of years. We would learn shortly it wouldn't go too far.

As Dad settled into his routine, we did too. Rose and I were relieved we didn't have to tell Dad we were putting him in a rest home because we couldn't take care of him anymore. He never asked us why he was there or when was he going home. Cristy said we were lucky. She said some patients fight it tooth and nail and make it hard on the family and the caregivers. All of us were grateful.

32

The Help

One of the things I had to learn was that a nursing home is not the Hilton or the Four Seasons. It's a nursing home. I knew that walking in, but I still had to learn it. It wasn't easy. Keeping Dad in there wasn't our first choice, but bringing him home wasn't an option anymore. Dad had to get used to his new home and so did we as his family.

They moved Dad and his roommate Larry to a permanent two-person room. Rose and I were glad they kept them together. We put pictures on the walls and did our best to make it feel as homey as possible. I think it was to make us feel better too.

When he was home, if he needed something, we could do it for him when he needed it done. He didn't have to wait. He was top priority, and we were there to serve him. But he wasn't home anymore, and we had to learn that the pecking order had changed. There were hundreds of other residents that wanted to be top priority too. But even with residents surrounding us in the halls, the lobby, the cafeteria, and their rooms, it didn't click that Dad was now one of the many and not number one anymore. Dad was the new kid on the block and so were we.

Some days I would come home frustrated because they took so long to come and change Dad, even after I went to the nurses' station. "They took forever to change Dad today," I'd tell Cristy. "I pushed the dang call button and it was like pushing all the buttons on a keyboard that don't do anything. What the heck?"

"Maybe they were short staffed today," she'd say, "or his CNA got called to another part of the facility."

It would frustrate me because it felt like she was sticking up for them all the time. What she was telling me made sense and sounded logical, but we were talking about Dad. *They should move him to the front of the line*, I would think, even though I knew it didn't work that way. But even though I didn't like the way Cristy stuck up for them, I knew she was speaking from experience. She knew exactly what she was talking about. She'd done it for twelve years. Lots of rules and methods had changed, but the human factor had not.

What she finally got through to me was that the families were people, the patients were people, and so were all the workers. I only considered the families' and the patient's point of view, but that was only part of the picture. It was like cracking a coconut, but she finally got to the part of my brain that listens. I finally realized that they didn't just work for Dad and the other residents, they worked for their own families at home. They had loved ones that were top priority too and were working there to keep their families moving forward.

Cristy gave me the best advice after the first few weeks Dad was there. One day I came home frustrated. She noticed it on my face when I came in the door. After thirty years of marriage, she can read me like a book — especially my face. "What's the matter?" she asked.

"Nothing."

"I can see it in your face."

"They left Dad too long in the wheelchair, he was slumped over asleep in it. They should have put him to bed. It bugs the crap out of me."

She walked over to our kitchen table and waved me over to sit by her. I complied.

"You have to remember," she said, "it's a nursing home, not an expensive hotel. The people that are taking care of your dad's basic needs are not paid that well, and remember, they're people too. The best thing you can do as a family member is to treat all the workers the best you possibly can. Get to know them and be considerate of their lives too. You can't be there all the time to stick up for your dad, but if you get to know them and show them that you care about their wellbeing too, they will make a connection between you and your dad. And when you're not around they will naturally take better care of him."

It took a little while for all that to sink in, but eventually it did. I made it a point to remember all the CNAs, charge nurses, housekeepers, and maintenance guys' names. I always asked them how they were doing and made an effort to get to know them. And guess what? Cristy was right. They were no different than me. They had their own ups and downs, money problems, family problems, joys, sorrows, and everything else in between. I can honestly say that I cared about all the workers I got to know at the nursing home. I still do. I appreciate what everyone did there, from the ones that mop the floors to the ones that write the checks.

There's an unmistakable feeling you get when you know someone cares about you. That's the feeling I got from a lot of the employees at Dad's nursing home. They not only cared about Dad, they cared about his family too. We are grateful.

33

The Land of the Misfits

Growing up, one of my favorite times of the year was Christmas. It always involved lots of family, fun, and not to mention presents. But one of my fondest memories about it was sitting with Mom, Dad, and Mary to watch *Rudolph the Red-Nosed Reindeer*. It was the greatest movie ever for Mary and me. We knew it only came on once a year and we only had one chance to see it. In those days there were no DVRs, DVDs, Netflix, or anything else. It was a one-shot deal, and we never missed it.

Whether we acknowledge it or even think about it, our quest in life is finding our place in this vast world and universe. We have this innate desire deep inside each one of us that wants to find its place to be nourished and grow. We all want to belong and matter. And we want to be in control of, as they say, our own destiny. But with age we see that there are many possibilities, many that we are in control of and some that we are not.

In chapter one I described the scene when I entered the nursing home as looking like a fifty-car pileup on the highway. I still have that image in my head. But it wasn't the first time I'd been in a nursing home. When Cristy and I first met, she was an LVN in a convalescent home connected to the hospital in town. I still remember going to visit her for lunch. I'd walked down the hall toward the nurses' station wanting to see her but wanting to get the heck out of there too. I was so uncomfortable. I wasn't used to seeing so many elderly people in wheelchairs and lying in beds. I would get the chills when one of the patients would yell out to me, "Hey, come here!" I didn't know what to do. I was more than a fish out of water. I still remember Cristy's smile as she walked toward me because she knew how uncomfortable I felt. She still laughs about it.

As time went on in Dad's new home, I got used to seeing people in wheelchairs with half their face drooped or their hands curled into a ball. I got used to seeing people with two or three teeth or none at all. I got used to patients wheeling into Dad's room because they couldn't find their own. It didn't make me uncomfortable anymore like when I was dating Cristy.

One day when I was visiting with Dad in the lobby, I looked around at all the faces that were now familiar to me. The lobby had a big TV against the wall with a DVD player connected to it. The residents congregated around it daily. Leonard, a resident, was in charge of putting the DVDs in. They had a bunch of old movies that they watched over and over. It was the highlight of most of their days. Most of them seemed like they weren't actually watching the movie, but they were there with their community enjoying the time out of their rooms. I remember one lady sat next to Leonard every day with a notepad and a pen. She would watch whatever movie was on intensely, and randomly she would lift her pen and pad and start writing. I never asked her what or why she did that for every movie she watched — even the ones she'd seen ten times. They all had different lives there, but they were all in the same place.

As I sat there that day, something hit me while I watched them watch the movie. Dad was sitting next to me in his wheelchair not really conscious of the movie playing in front of him. I looked around at all the residents around me, and it reminded me of *Rudolph the Red-Nosed Reindeer*. It wasn't on the TV, but I realized something looking around. I was in the Land of the Misfits, and Dad lived there now. He was in a place that no one chooses to go.

The people were like the toys on the island: broken, missing parts, and not functioning properly. They were separated from the everyday living we all enjoy. Limitations surrounded them, both their own and those of the land they were living in. Not one of them said, "Hey, I think I'd like to live here confined to a wheelchair or a bed." Not one of them wanted people changing or showering them. But this was the lot they were living. It was where life and circumstance had put them.

With time I got more comfortable and started to meet more and more residents and something became crystal clear to me: Each one of them is a whole person. They are not misfits. Each one has lived a life, with its ups and downs, jagged edges, sorrows, and great joys. And just like Dad, they all have a story to be told.

34

Gold in His Hands

Thanksgiving 2018 came, and Dad was still hanging in there — so to speak. I wasn't sure if I should try and take him out of the nursing home to eat with the family. I brought him home for Easter, and he wasn't happy. I tried everything to get him to smile, but nothing worked. We had trouble getting him in the car, and out. My home is not handicap friendly, so everything was a battle. After I got him back to the facility that day, I swore I would never put him, or myself, through that again. My first thought was "I'm not going to try that again," but my heart told me, "You need to try." I did, and we all had a great time. My brother-in-law's house was perfect for a handicapped person. Dad had a good time surrounded by his family. We ate good food together, and Dad got to see his two new great-grandchildren. It was a perfect day.

Christmas 2018 seemed to pop up the day after

Thanksgiving. That's how it felt, anyway. But I didn't have to make the decision of whether to bring Dad home for Christmas or not. Starting about two weeks before Christmas, Dad really slowed down. His appetite was gone. We had to downgrade him to pureed food because his chewing and swallowing capabilities diminished in just a few days. His eyes opened less and less, and when they were open, they looked dim. I tried everything to get him to laugh or smile. I'd shave him to try and perk him up. He loved me telling him how handsome he was in the mirror, but that didn't work either.

"He won't eat," Rose would tell me.

"Don't worry, he has plenty to live off of," I would say patting his stomach, trying not to face the inevitable. We both knew what was happening but didn't say a word.

My two nephews, my niece, and my son would be coming into town with their families for Christmas. I was anxious for all of them to come. I wanted them to see their grandpa because I didn't think he would be here for the next holiday.

It was the Sunday before Christmas, and my daughter Sara and I went to go see Dad. He was in a wheelchair sleeping. "Hi, Dad, it's me and Sara." No response. "Dad! Wake up, Dad," I said, not frantically, but louder to wake him. His eyes barely cracked open. "How 'bout we give you a little shave to perk you up, Dad?"

No response.

I got his shaving gear and rolled him into his bathroom. Sara followed with the towels. The sun was out, shining through the sliding glass door next to his bed. I wrapped him up with the towels and started shaving. Sara and I talked to him and told him how good he looked and that he was the most handsome guy in the world. He always liked that. I knew he was awake because he gave me a few sighs of satisfaction while I glided the razor down his cheeks.

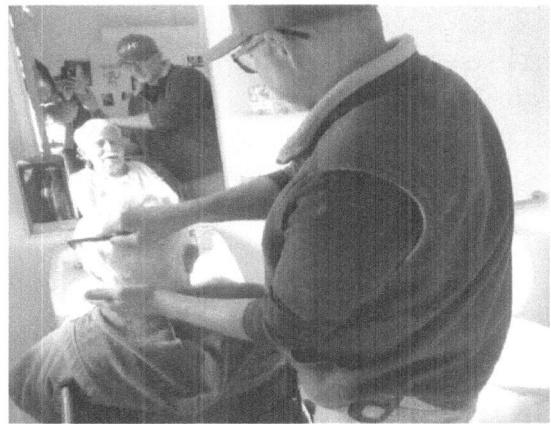

While I shaved him, I told him, "Dad, I just want you to know that if you're ready to go home, we'll be okay. Don't worry about us, we know where you'll be. And we'll see you again."

Sara confirmed what I said. "It's okay if you want to go home, Grandpa, we love you. We'll be okay."

He gave no response, but we knew he heard us.

I talked to all the kids that day and asked them if we could all meet there on Christmas Eve at the nursing home. I told them that Grandpa might not be with us much longer. We managed to get there at the same time and have a nice visit with him. He didn't open his eyes but for a few glimpses he shared with us. We knew he was awake because he gave sighs of agreement and a couple of small smiles. I was glad they all made it to see him. I didn't know how much longer he had, tomorrow hadn't revealed itself yet.

Christmas Eve came, we had the food, we had the family at our place, and all seemed to be normal. Kids played; we had our traditional family bingo game with presents for prizes. But something was missing. I felt it all night, like something was out of sorts. Even though it seemed like everyone was having a good time, I was a little sick inside.

The last of the family left around 11:30 that evening. The house looked like someone had detonated a bomb inside. A happy mess, I guess. But I had an odd sense of pent-up nervous energy that I needed to do something with. I told Cristy I knew it was late but I didn't want to wake up to a messy house. She agreed. We started cleaning and she walked up to me and said, "Did you feel like something was off tonight, like something wasn't right?"

She took the words right out of my mouth. "I feel the same way," I told her. "I feel like we had a good time, but not really."

She agreed, and we kept cleaning until 2 a.m. trying to work the kink out of our emotions. We didn't know the reason why we felt that way, but there is a reason for everything.

The day after Christmas, I woke up at my normal time, 4 a.m., and I had this feeling that I needed to go to Dad's house and do his yard. It had only been a couple of weeks since I did it last, and nothing had really grown, but I couldn't shake the feeling. "You need to go do your dad's yard," I kept hearing in my head (not literally).

If the sun had been out at 4 a.m. I probably would have gone and did the yard. At 5:30 a.m., Cristy got up and I told her I was going to do Dad's yard as soon as the sun came up. "I have to do it. It needs to be done today."

As I've mentioned before, a big part of Dad's life was his yard. He loved going out and doing something every day to keep it looking loved. When I took over his duties because he couldn't do them anymore, he would come out and sit on a piece of wood and watch me mow his lawn or trim his bushes. He was never too shy to tell me I missed something either.

I would tell him, "You trying to kill me?"

He would laugh, "Maybe."

If you looked up their address on Google still today there's an image of Dad's front yard with me mowing and him sitting on the piece of wood watching me.

As I write about this part of his life, the keys on the keyboard seem harder to press because I know where they're headed.

I went and did Dad's yard. Rose wasn't home, she spent the night at her son's place. It was a nice, clear day. I took my time and did an extra nice job, one Dad would be proud of. After I finished, I went to go see him to make sure he was all shaved up for the day. They had already shaved him, and he was still in bed. I tried to wake him, but his eyes stayed shut. He only gave me a couple of sighs and a light moan. I stayed there a while and talked to his closed eyes and told him I would be back for dinner.

I went back to relieve Rose at 5:30 p.m. She did dinner that day, and I was going to do bedtime. We called it dinner and a movie. I walked into the room and Rose was sitting at the foot of the bed. "He won't wake up and he won't eat," she said.

I walked over and ran my fingers through his soft

grey hair. I loved telling him he looked like a movie star and that he had million-dollar hair. He liked it too. "He looks peaceful," I told her.

There was something about him that evening. He had an unmistakable look, one of a person at perfect peace. He had a look of satisfaction that needed no words. Any description I could give would not accurately describe what emanated from him. I kept telling Rose, "I can't believe how peaceful he looks."

Looking back now I realize how profound that moment was: A man who lived his whole life to get to that point. Complete peace.

Rose motioned me off to the side and told me softly, "I told your dad that if he was ready to go, to not worry about me, that I would be okay. I told him to go see his Sara."

What a wonderful, unselfish person she is, was the first thought that crossed my mind.

Rose walked to the left side of his bed and ran her hand down his cheek. "I'm going to go home now, honey. I'll be back at lunchtime tomorrow, okay?"

I was standing on the other side of the bed and watched him turn his head toward her and open his eyes wide open, something he hadn't done in a couple of weeks. He reached out and held her hand and looked into her eyes saying no words that said everything. He thanked her, he told her he loved her, and he told her he would see her again one day, using every last ounce of energy he had. He closed his eyes.

Rose left for the evening and I stayed and sat on his bed holding his hand. Just me and Dad.

I sat looking at the peaceful look on his face. His

mustache looked perfect, like someone had spent hours placing each hair perfectly, one next to the other and cut to perfection.

It reminded me of being a kid one day in San Jose. I'm not sure how old I was, but Mom called out, "Dad's home."

I ran to the front door and opened it. I stepped back. "Hi, son," the man said.

I stepped back farther. "You're not my dad," I said, looking up at the man with no mustache.

"It's me, *Mijo*," he said.

"You're not my dad! Mom!" I yelled, starting to cry.

He knelt down and smiled and pointed to the gap between his two front teeth, "Remember these bucket seats?"

I realized it was him and calmed down.

He waved me over and promised me he wouldn't shave his mustache off ever again. I was satisfied. I don't think I ever saw him without one since then.

But it reminded me of the promise he and Mom made to each other when they were a young couple with two young children: That their lives would be different, that God and family were number one, and that they wouldn't pass on to Mary and me any of the baggage they had to carry around when they were young. He kept his promise.

I sat with him for a little longer and told him softly in his ear before I left, "I love you, Pop. I'll see you tomorrow."

I went home to pick up some paint brushes. I was going over to the house I grew up in to paint the washroom. They were going to deliver a washer and dryer the next day.

Cristy walked up to me. "I want to go see your dad," she told me.

"He's asleep, go tomorrow."

"I want to see him. Sara and I are going," she said.

"Okay, I'll be at the old house painting." I figured there was no sense in arguing. Once she's made up her mind, it's made.

My Bluetooth speaker was singing mariachi music throughout the house while I was painting. It's something I woke up to every morning growing up, the music playing, the sound of food sizzling over the stove, and the aroma of homemade flour tortillas drawing me in. I used to get up extra early just to have them hot off the press. Tortillas with butter, they are the best. I can still hear Mom singing along and talking with Dad as she cooked.

When I was almost done painting, I heard someone bang through the front door and call out, "Babe! Dad!" It was Sara and Cristy. "We heard a song on the way over here, it was beautiful. It kept saying, "Welcome, welcome good and faithful servant, you have done well," Sara said, as excited as I've ever seen her. They went on and on about how beautiful it was. "That was for your dad," Cristy said.

Cristy told me while I was painting that she told Dad if he wanted to go home that I would be okay, and that she would take care of me. I finished around 10 p.m. We went home and I took a shower and as I was putting on my pajamas my phone rang. The screen showed ROSE on it. I knew the call I was answering before I swiped across the screen.

"The nursing home just called," she said. "Your dad just passed."

Oh, poor Dad, I thought. "We'll be right there to pick you up," I told her. Cristy, Sara, and I picked her up and rode silently with the image of Dad lying in his bed with a silent heart in our minds.

We walked down the hallway toward his room. Larry, his roommate, was just outside his room sobbing. He had grown to love Dad, just like the rest of us. "I'll be there with him soon," he told us between breaths.

We walked in and Dad lay in his quietest state, waiting to hear what his loved ones might say at his bedside. He looked as peaceful as he did earlier that evening, except he had a towel rolled up tight, tucked under his chin keeping his mouth closed. No more words to be spoken by him, only the life he lived could do that for him now.

Within a half hour it became a family affair. My nephew Vicente, my mother and father-in-law, my brother-in-law and his wife, and Rose's son and daughter came. We surrounded his bed and talked and laughed about the man that lay in front of us. Nobody was sobbing, nobody was shouting, *Why? Why did you have to take him?* It was what he wanted.

I was standing next to him running my fingers through his million-dollar hair like I always did. I glided the backs of my fingers down his cheeks as they cooled. We stayed and talked around him for almost two hours. It wasn't a sad gathering; it was a peaceful celebration.

One day when Dad was still home, I was sitting with him in his living room watching a movie. I could see him shaking his head in the corner of my eye. I lowered the volume on the TV. "What's wrong, Dad?" I asked him.

He put his hands out, palms up. "I feel so bad, son. I feel so bad you and Rose have to take care of me," he said, like he was disgusted with himself.

I reached over and put my hand on his arm. "Don't worry, Dad, that's what we're here for. We love you."

He reached out to me with his palm up and said, "Son, you are like a precious piece of gold in my hand," tapping his palm with the other. "You are precious gold, son,"

I tell you this story because as we stood around Dad that night it came to mind. It was fitting. I believe at the moment of Dad's last heartbeat, God reached down and put him in the palm of his hand like a precious piece of gold, a precious son, and took him to Himself.

35

Period

My alarm went off at 4 a.m. like every day. I got the coffee going and set up my little workstation. A long coffee table in our family room where I stack my books, my Bible, and my moleskine notebooks I write in before the words click their way onto the page. I sat on the loveseat that has molded itself to my body over the years. My routine is the same every day. I read my daily Bible readings, I read something on writing, and, lastly, I write. If I don't start my day that way, my whole day is off. It's like leaving the house with two different shoes on, it just doesn't feel right. I say that because I did that once as an adult. It taught me that it's not always wise to dress in the dark.

But this day was different. It was January 4, 2018 the day of Dad's funeral. It would be our final goodbye and mark the end of a life. I read my Bible and wrote a partial chapter for this book that morning, still moving forward, what Dad would have wanted.

All week long all of us prayed that everything would go well for the funeral, that there wouldn't be any hiccups. I walked outside about 7 a.m. and the sky was crystal clear, just a few thin strips of clouds accenting the blue canvas behind them. It wasn't cold, it was a perfect day.

We pulled up to Sacred Heart Church, where Dad's last day would begin. The church was full, not an empty seat. A testimony to the man that lay at the foot of the altar. The service was more than I could have prayed for. When the final song played and we were following Dad in the casket down the center of the church, I felt a sense of pride seeing every pew packed tightly with people that loved Dad watching him roll by. All of them were a part of his story. What more could a person ask for? To be loved because they have given love. The holy grail.

It was a never-ending line of cars and trucks following the white hearse that held Dad. It was about 11:30 a.m. by the time everyone got to the cemetery. Jumbled in groups, people were talking and slowly making their way toward the burial site. The sun was glistening bright with transparent puffs of clouds moving slowly by, we couldn't have asked for a more beautiful day.

Our local priest, Fr. Ken, read the final words to aid Dad on his journey as we sat on those uncomfortable funeral chairs they have for the family. I don't like them, because if you are in one it's probably because you lost someone.

The ceremony continued, and the Honor Guard came and gave Dad some last words. They asked that we all stand in honor of Dad and asked ex-military to salute and everyone else to place their hands on their hearts.

I looked around and salutes speckled the crowd. It was a proud moment. Like a boom, the first volley of shots went off. Everyone jumped, I mean everyone. They caught us off guard. If it wasn't a funeral it would have been funny. We all knew there were two more volleys coming. We were prepared. When those shots went off, it was the most exhilarating moment I think I've ever lived. It was like a rocket soaring off in the midst of us. It marked the end of a good life. A novel that was started on September 27, 1935 and finished on December 26, 2017. That last round of shots was the satisfying, profound period an author puts after the last sentence on the last page of a good story, knowing that it continues in the hearts and minds of those who have read it.

The Secret

"The secret to life is knowing how it will end"

While writing my way through Dad's life, the quote above, which is also on the front cover of this book, popped into my mind. I doubt I'm the first person to ever come up with it. I believe everything has been thought, spoken, and written at one time or another throughout history, but this is my twist on it.

The quote moved me; I loved the way it sounded. Mysterious. A secret for sure, but I couldn't see how it related to Dad. He didn't know how his life would end, or on what day it would happen. Who knows that? *Nobody*, I thought. But as many will tell you, perspective is everything. In every aspect of life, lack of knowledge and lack of perspective blinds us to the truths that are out there for all to understand.

A few years back I was driving down the road and a song came on the radio. It was in between 7 and 9 a.m. in the morning. I know that because the station I was listening to plays Mariachi music in that timeslot every day. There was something special about it. It moved me. The main chorus line was "*Soy tan feliz* (I'm so happy)." It sounded *so* beautiful to me.

Music is more than just notes, and more than just entertainment. It can be healing, and uplifting. It can unlock a part of us that transcends our human limits. It is a vehicle that can take us back to places we have been before, and one that can transport us to places we have never been.

I pulled over and whipped my iPhone out and opened the iTunes app. *I have to have it,* I thought. But I couldn't find it. The song kept repeating the chorus line, "*Soy Tan Feliz.*" I wanted it. But it was as if someone didn't want me to find it yet. It was meant for another time.

I looked for it a few times after that day with no luck and would eventually forget about the song. But on June 6, 2018, a few years later, and six months after Dad's passing, I heard it again. It was 7:30 a.m., and I was in Strathmore, California, driving down the road with Mariachi music on, like always. And just like the first time, on the same station, the song came on the radio. But this time I had the Shazam app. I pulled over like the first time and opened the app and let it listen to the song, and sure enough, "*Parece que fue ayer* (It seems like yesterday)," by Ezequiel Peña, appeared on the screen. That was the name of the song.

I downloaded it and set it to repeat. I pressed play and pulled back onto the road. As I went down the road listening to the song, I could feel something welling up inside. I hadn't shed many tears for Dad since he died, because I knew he was exactly where he wanted to be. But on that day, driving down the road listening to that song, it hit me. A wave of emotion crashed through me, like nothing I had ever felt. Every time the chorus line in the song said those words, *"Soy tan feliz,"* more tears pulsed down my cheeks. Tears of joy.

In John 15:12 Jesus says, "My command is this: Love each other as I have loved you."

In that moment I was granted a speck of what Jesus meant. I felt the love of which He speaks. Great Love. It's bigger than what we know here on earth. We can strive for it, but it can only be perfected on our last day. I felt it, just for a moment. The love Dad, Mom, and Mary were living. That indescribable love that we all hope to share one day. A miracle for sure.

I finally understood how Dad could know how his life would end. He knew the secret to life was the human heart, where the real treasure lies. A powerful, mysterious force that can move people to do great things.

He knew the secret was more than just an answer or a solution. It was a desire, not a place or a time when he would take his last breath. It was a decision anyone can make any time in their life. To know God. He made that choice; he solved the mystery. It didn't matter what day his heart took its last beat, because he knew that matters of the heart were more than just a day. And he knew with God in it, his end was merely the beginning.

To my Sis
Maria Dolores Rincon

The picture above on the right is a snapshot of a moment in time that reminds me of my relationship with Mary. She was my big sister. Growing up we laughed, we played and were always together. But she was also my tormenter. I was her number one target, but I think I kind of loved it – if that makes any sense. I remember running with her to the best rides in Disneyland and the excitement we shared and seeing Dad and Mom waiting with smiles on their faces, happy that their kids were happy. I remember Mom and Dad letting us stay up as late as we wanted on the weekends in San Jose baking cakes at 1:00 a.m. in the morning watching the old Wolfman and Frankenstein movies and then being afraid to sleep by myself. She would let me sleep in her room, but it came with a price. I had to kiss her feet before I got into her bed. I'm not kidding. I told you she was my tormenter. But it must not have been too bad, because I always came back for more. She will always be my big sister.

The picture above on the left is the image I have of her as a woman. A strong woman. She had a strength about her. A drive that took me years to understand. She always knew what she wanted, and nothing was going to stop her. She was one of those people that once they set their mind to something, it's their only destination. The amazing thing is that she did most of it after marrying – kids and all. Sometimes I would think: *Slow down Sis, I think you've accomplished enough.*

Not many of us ever find that one thing that we love to do. Something we're obsessed with; something we have to do in our lifetime. It's not about money, it's about meaning. Mary loved working with patients in the hospitals she worked in, and loved teaching nursing students how to be the best they could be in any situation. She found that illusive gold nugget that many search for their whole life and never find: what we truly love to do.

I don't think I would have ever found the gold nugget in my life and pursued it without Mary's example. I love to write. I am grateful for the life she shared with me and look forward to the day we meet again.

I Love You Sis

To the Reader

One thing you learn in life is that the older you get the faster time seems to go by. It seems like we walked into kindergarten, then leapfrogged to high school, then got transported to being fifty, sixty, or whatever age we might be. It's kind of scary. But with age we realize – if we're lucky – if we appreciate the time we have today and use it wisely, tomorrow will always be better.

The goal of any writer is to connect with the reader. And the only way to do that is to cross paths with them; to intersect with their lives with the words you lay on the page. Pictures help, but the words are the road people travel to reach the message. I can't relate to a millionaire, because I'm not one. But if the millionaire lost a son, daughter, mother, or father in a tragic accident, or is taking care of a sick parent, we are on common ground. Whether I'm picking fruit for a living, or wearing a three-piece suit on wall street, we can relate to each other, because we share something where money has no relevance, and our lives have intersected. Our shared humanity has brought us together. I hope that we have crossed paths, and our lives have intersected, and that the message was clear. And I hope that you found some gold nuggets to take with you for your own journey, and for the precious time you spent reading our story. I am grateful, and I know Dad would be humbled to know you spent time out of your life to know his.

God Bless
Robert

Special Thanks

I would like to thank all those who were willing to take time out of their busy lives to read the early drafts of this book, and for the priceless feedback they gave me. I am so grateful.

Grandpa Mike
Grandma Mia
Tia Josie
Rose
Andy
Elizabeth
Lupita
Christine
My Sara
Terese

Matt
Juan
Bobby

Thank You

www.ingramcontent.com/pod-product-compliance
Lightning Source LLC
Chambersburg PA
CBHW030908080526
44589CB00010B/200